HOW TO write and PUBLISH YOUR family STORY

in 10 easy steps

NOELINE KYLE has published widely in the fields of women's history, biography and family history. She has been recognised nationally and internationally as an expert on writing and publishing family history for more than thirty years. Family historians, local family history groups, state and national genealogical societies and historical societies regularly seek her advice and expertise, which means she is often on the road, giving workshops and seminars. She is an honorary professor at the University of Sydney and emeritus professor of Queensland University of Technology. Noeline is the author of *We Should've Listened to Grandma: Women and family history* (1988), *Tracing Family History in Australia* (1985), *The Family History Writing Book* (1993), and *Writing Family History Made Very Easy* (2007).

HOW TO write and PUBLISH YOUR family STORY

in 10 easy steps

Noeline Kyle

NEWSOUTH

My thanks to Phillipa McGuinness and all at NewSouth Publishing, and especially to Melita Rogowsky and the editors Emma Driver and Marie-Louise Taylor, who gently alerted me to errors and omissions and who helped to shape my unruly text into this useful book on writing and publishing family stories.

A NewSouth book

Published by
NewSouth Publishing
University of New South Wales Press Ltd
University of New South Wales
Sydney NSW 2052
AUSTRALIA
www.newsouthpublishing.com.au

© Noeline Kyle 2011
First published 2011

10   9   8   7   6   5   4   3   2   1

National Library of Australia
Cataloguing-in-Publication entry
  Author: Kyle, Noeline, 1940–
  Title: How to write and publish your family story in ten easy steps/by
    Noeline Kyle.
  ISBN: 9 781 74223 275 1 (pbk.)
  Subjects: Genealogy.
    Genealogy – Authorship.
    Genealogical literature – Publishing.
    Australia – Genealogy – Handbooks, manuals, etc.
  Dewey Number: 929.1072094

Design Josephine Pajor-Markus
Cover design Design by Committee
Cover images SXC
Printer Ligare

This book is printed on paper using fibre supplied from plantation or sustainably managed forests.

Contents

Before you start...

For over thirty years, in country towns from Nowra to Nambucca Heads and in the Central West of New South Wales, in libraries, town halls, conference centres, universities and in local meeting rooms, I have met and taught people trying to tell their stories. We have laughed and cried our way through stories of birth, death, disappointment, great moments of joy, discovery, journeys of life and how our ancestors – our grandparents and great grandparents – journeyed across the world, were married, created families and grew old. This book is a culmination of the many writing journeys I have encountered along the way. It is a book that answers many of the questions each of us face as writers. It is a book that emphatically says that you *can* write and publish your own story, and, with the help of e-publishing and e-book technologies, there are now many more ways that you can get on with it. I have benefited greatly from talking to the thousands of students I have met and taught. It has been an enthralling, marvellous journey and I thank every one of you.

You've decided to be the family historian, and you've made good progress on researching the details of your family's story. Now it is time to think about writing and publishing your work. This book offers practical steps in the writing, formatting and shaping of a book manuscript and eases you through the many and varied tasks associated with self-publishing and book promotion, including the 'how-to' of e-books and e-publishing. There is no doubt that technological change is revolutionising the way you can write, edit, publish and promote a book. At the time of going to press all quoted websites, sources and specific advice are current and have been carefully checked for their veracity. But inevitably commentary on software, URLs and current technologies will soon be out-of-date. At the same time I have made considerable effort to outline universal practical steps that will continue to be useful for a very long time. Writing, editing, publishing and promoting family stories is about more than technology of course and this book garners together over thirty years of writing and publishing experience by the author – as a professional historian, family historian and published writer – to propose straightforward, useful and accessible strategies for getting your family story into print.

Noeline Kyle

Getting started

Writing and publishing a family story is a challenging, exhilarating and creative enterprise – but it can be a daunting task for the novice.

Ask for help. Become a member of your local family history society. Make every effort to talk to local and family historians in your community. Research how other writers go about their writing and publishing.

Join a writing group. Take part in and visit local and family history research rooms. Search out local printers and digital publishers. Study how others write and publish their books.

The latest versions of genealogy software and other writing software have templates and designs to assist you to construct a 'book' – with these you can collate charts, insert biographical data and images, and add a contents list. However, such software cannot write, edit or publish the book for you. That task finally rests with you. And it is a very worthwhile task – preserving your family story in the portable, accessible and relatively inexpensive format of a book allows generations of family members to know their history.

Things to think about

Each chapter in this book presents a series of easy-to-follow steps to help you move from researching and writing your family story to the final printing and publication of a book. It is written with the novice writer/self-publisher in mind, although more advanced researcher/writers will also find it useful. The book introduces the reader to the concepts and strategies offered by new technology but does not ignore traditional means of getting your family story into print.

Some of the issues you face as a self-publisher include grappling with editing; proofreading; page layout; and inserting images, maps and charts. You will need to think about how to construct chapters and choose a title. You will make decisions about what to put in, and what to leave out of the many stories that make up your family's narrative. You will ponder over the writing of biographical entries, trying to ensure they are historically authentic and textually pleasing but often unsure about how to do this. The ever-changing technological maze of self-publishing may at times overwhelm you as you try to shape your family story and, at the same time, make it fit the actual page.

Family historians generally have been quick to use digital technology, the Internet and email. It has been their sustained and meticulous research into and use of early historical records and primary documentary research that has fostered and underpinned the development of online indexes, increased accessibility to state records for all researchers, and the use of computers, printers and new software for recording, writing and producing family history. And, like all writers, family historians have had to keep in touch with changes in book production, as e-book technology and handheld readers enter the market.

Publishing family stories, local history, autobiography, biography, memoir, travel stories and much more via the Internet, on DVD, CD or video, and via other social media is increasingly popular, especially among younger writers. Nonetheless, the physical book has remained a publishing medium of choice for the family historian and for writers in other genres. It is unlikely this will change, although you can add the e-book to the range of possibilities you consider for getting your family story into print.

This book demystifies the process of how to get your family story published. It has practical advice drawn from more than thirty years of my work with family and local historians, and teaching classes on how to write, edit, construct stories and publish family stories, memoir and local history. Indeed there are a great number of different ways of writing and publishing your story and I canvass them throughout this book. And whether you make the decision to stay with a printed book, publish online or create an e-book, you will continue to construct your text in such a way as to appeal to your reader.

The chronicler of family stories begins the writing and publishing journey with many years of research. I have written at length about how historians are drawn to and begin to enjoy this research process. It is one of the most satisfying and personally rewarding tasks you can do. Who wouldn't be excited by the prospect of finding out the fascinating and often intriguing data you discover about your family? How often have you waited with bated breath as your search of an immigration index downloads its precious results? And that skip of a heartbeat as you see for the first time your name, your family name, there in the records telling you so much about the past?

But as much as you love the research, it is not enough. At some point, you will take up your pen and write, and the earlier you do that in the research process the easier the writing will be. Writing as you research is the way to go: if you begin your writing as early as possible, your ability and confidence will improve over time so that you will be better prepared to write the final draft of your book. Further, writing at the same time as you do the research will ensure your research is more focused and more useful for your later history writing, editing and publishing.

'Ah yes,' you might say, 'but in what way do I write, and how do I get started?' In my earlier book *Writing Family History Made Very Easy* I list specific strategies for getting started with the writing process, and I discuss at length how to write more authentically and vibrantly about characters. I provide advice on how to choose a format and I tell the reader that asking questions, critical questions, leads to the best kind of family story writing. I include strategies and writing exercises for the novice as well as the more advanced writer.

In this book, I take you a step further and map out the strategies to shape your stories, your family memories and your biographies into that bigger story: your family history. In other words, this book is a practical guide to how you move through and from your research, your writing, your ideas and your collected photographs, maps and charts to construct a manuscript that will be readable, interesting and ready for the printer or publisher.

Since the late 1970s, there has been substantial growth in online indexes, increased use of the Internet for the quick downloading of advice and information, and many developments in technologies that support writing and publishing at home. It is relatively easy today to find the software you need to help put together your chapters and there is a plethora of programs, ranging from free or inexpensive software through to the expensive industry standards such as InDesign, QuarkXPress or PageMaker, to help with page layout, scanning images and constructing a book. Nonetheless, despite advances in editing, printing and publishing technology the old adage remains: rubbish in, rubbish out! Your writing and your final story will only work if you take the trouble to construct your text in a credible, interesting way. This book will help you sort through your many ideas and your proposed family story to find the best way to shape your story and produce your book.

Publishing a family story is a unique process. However, it has at its heart a challenge familiar to most writers: how to rein in and shape a coherent story out of the overabundance of collected data now residing on our desks, in our computers and even under our beds! In this book I focus on constructing a family story – a family history – from a range of source material. However, this model or template can be used to write a memoir, a local history, a story of a business or indeed an account of a personal journey. All of these formats are being used by family historians and all are underpinned by a wide range of family history research.

Know your audience

Before you can begin to construct your story, choose a format and get it in shape, you might ask the question: who am I writing for? The answer will help you decide how to begin the task of planning your book and getting it into print.

There is no doubt most of us write to be read. You write stories for family, knowing that they will be your readers; if you are writing a local history, your readers can extend to a wider range of readers in the community. Some life stories have a universal appeal – they may resonate with people who have lived through a particular historical period or event such as a world war or an economic depression. It's important to start thinking about these things early in the research and writing process, and to arrive at some answers well before you write your final draft.

Nevertheless, no matter how widely your story is to be read it is your project too. What kind of family story do you want to write and see in print? You may be writing a family history to coincide with a parent's 80th birthday celebration, a family anniversary or a family reunion, and in that case the format of your book may tend toward a traditional (linear or chronological) structure. If you prefer to record the story of a favourite character, a biographical format might appeal.

Are you looking for a genetic link to the past? Do you look at your grandchildren and recognise aspects of yourself when you were young? Who else in that ancestral past might have had similar characteristics? I have many strong women in my family. My mother steeled herself and left a broken, dangerous marriage in 1956. Her life thereafter was testament to her as a woman of courage, character and fierce determination to succeed. Her grandmother became a single parent in 1890 when she told her feckless Irish husband to go after he had gambled away a baby's layette. Who else in my past could have been like that? There are patterns of character, behaviour, occupation, talent and relationships which emerge in a family and I am constantly surprised by the stories family historians tell me about this. We all want to find an answer to these questions of likenesses, hopes and dreams which filter down the generations to surprise us even today.

Do you have a puzzle to solve? Is there a crime, a secret or a strange event that continues to haunt the family? In chapter 9 of this book I outline the privacy and ethics issues you will need to address if you intend to include sensitive or debatable information in your stories. A case of bigamy, family breakdown or family dysfunction in the distant past may have little impact on descendants today. However, it is wise to check with individuals or family members who retain both familial and emotional links to that past because their feelings about exposure may differ markedly from your own.

The answers to all these questions will determine how you go about approaching the final layout, design and construction of your book.

The first steps

Before you start, consider the following:

» Talk to other family historians about how they go about constructing, editing, writing and designing their family stories.

» Join a local family history or local historical society and check out their resources; attend their meetings and listen to the stories members tell about their experiences of researching, writing and publishing family stories.

» Research printers and publishers in your area. Digital printers can be found in the Yellow Pages and you will find lists on the Internet, at libraries and in publications on how to write and publish books.

What you will need

Make sure you have access to the equipment and software programs you will need:

» *Computer and printer.* Unless you are proficient in the use of advanced scanning, printing and editing technology it is not necessary to purchase anything other than a standard PC or Mac computer for word processing, editing and generally working on your text. If, like me, you prefer to print out the text for revision and editing, a black and white laser printer is economical. However, if you require some colour reproduction the newer model inkjet printers are adequate for printing photographs and other material for your own use.

» *Scanner and digital camera.* A digital camera can be used to photograph family members, documents that provide interesting illustrations throughout your text, and context images (of landscape, houses and other buildings, and workplaces). You can scan photographs and documents to file with a flatbed scanner or multifunction printer. Chapter 7 has more advice on scanning, inserting and choosing images for your book.

» *USB memory stick, flash drive or external hard drive.* You will need enough memory to store back-up files, your completed manuscript, images and additional research material.

» *Software.* A copy of Microsoft Word and software such as Photoshop Elements or PaintShop Photo Pro for editing and manipulating your images are adequate for the self-publisher. Genealogy software is widely used for storing and recording the large amounts of data collected. You will find advice on how these can help with the writing and publishing process in chapter 2 (Formatting lives) and chapter 8 (Electronic and paper publishing).

If you are not confident using computing technology and other digital devices it is best to leave much of the above to your printer or digital publisher. Make initial approaches to several local printers and talk to other writers of family stories such as family historians, local historians and local published writers so that you have a good knowledge of what you will have to do to get your family history into print. I have self-published two family histories and several other books and with advances in digital technology it has become much more possible for the amateur to do these tasks.

However, there are complex processes involved and as the researcher, writer and now self-publisher of your book there are specific steps to take and questions to ask yourself before you start. Let's begin.

Useful websites

The following websites can help you sort through the many issues you face as a writer and self-publisher. They offer advice and free downloads on how to find an agent, useful resources, style guides, rates of pay for writers, funding opportunities and tips on getting published:

Association of Authors' Representatives, Inc.
(United States)
<http://aaronline.org>
Australian Society of Authors
<www.asauthors.org>
Canadian Authors Association Writing Guides &
Newsletters
<www.canauthors.org/links/general.html>
WritersServices (United Kingdom)

2

Formatting lives

Organising your text into a credible, readable and appealing family story is the next step for turning your manuscript into a book.

It is not mandatory that you include long lists of names and dates simply because you have collected them. There are different and distinctive ways of organising paragraphs, chapters, sections, stories. However, each paragraph should flow easily into the next one, and each story and chapter should fit well with those before and after it.

Write a family story that others, and especially your family, will want to read and which is clearly set out, authentic and easy to read.

Your family will be the prime market and it makes sense to test your ideas on them as early in the process as possible. Perhaps they'll suggest alternative ways of arranging your narrative.

Constructing lives

In the early stages of writing family history, one of the main tasks is working out where individuals, families and generations fit together. This is also true when writing any history, biography or memoir. Genealogy software can be helpful here allowing you to print out individual charts, family charts or trees and lists of names and dates. Such software is very useful for sorting out errors in dates, eliminating duplication and generally fixing the glitches that creep into record keeping over the years.

In a recent self-published family history I made every effort to present my generations so as to make them readable. I think I did succeed but I was surprised when individuals, on a first reading, found some family relationships complex and difficult to understand. What this taught me was that although names, dates and events become very familiar to the author of any family story, readers will never spend the same amount of time perusing the text. At most they will carefully read the entry relating to their parents and grandparents or read the stories of familiar individuals and families. Therefore, as the family chronicler you should keep this in mind as you decide on a structure for the book.

The trick is to construct your family stories in such a way as to make the data accessible and comprehensible to readers who are not as familiar with it. This advice is true for other genres too, such as memoir, biography, travel writing or local history. As researchers and writers, we become very familiar with the many characters, complex relationships, places and events, but we sometimes forget that readers can find such detail confusing.

Your readers will need signposts and/or sensible explanations to ease them into the text. Classic novels such as William Makepeace Thackeray's *Vanity Fair* contain innumerable major and minor characters and a great many plot lines. It is easy for the reader to become lost although most of us will keep reading. It is likely your readers will not be as persistent as Thackeray's, however, and you will need to make a real effort to guide them through your text.

Use simple headings with the names of individual families or generations to guide the reader, place short charts at the beginning of chapters for readers' information and ensure biographical material is straightforward and easy to follow. Four essential starting points for your text are:

1   Keep it straightforward and easy to follow.
2   Ensure it is readable.
3   Organise your information in a logical way.
4   Use signposts (sensible explanations) to ease your
    readers into the text.

Build your family story around a character, use chronology to your advantage and write with passion about the lives, events and dramatic family relationships that begin to populate the pages of your book.

Parallel lives

I wrote my first family history as a biography (*Memories & Dreams: A biography of Nurse Mary Kirkpatrick*) and recently completed a biography/family story of a woman who as an adolescent confessed to a brutal crime (*A Greater Guilt: Constance Emilie Kent and the road murder*). I find biography very useful as a format for shaping a family story. A biography provides the focus (on a character) that we need to shape the story and, at the same time, the format allows the author to bring in the characters, events and intersecting stories of other family members. These other or parallel lives enliven the text, enrich and deepen the story line, provide interest (through conflict, contrast or difference) and lead to a greater understanding of what kind of story we should be constructing.

You can observe parallel stories being used in television series such as *Law & Order* and *The Bill*, when two or more story lines run parallel to each other, and the scenes alternate between the various stories being told. It is a technique you will unconsciously adopt when writing about one ancestor – say, a great grandfather – and you realise that to provide a complete picture, you must write about his wife (your great grandmother) before they met and married. You then bring these lives together and write about them as a couple.

Your ancestors lived in close-knit extended families and communities. Unlike today, these were communities where friendships and acquaintances were important for social, economic and political survival. This gives you scope to explore and explain the various relationships among family and community members. And so your family story begins to take on a depth and richness, revealing small pieces of family life as well as family and community intersections that might not have occurred to you at first.

Creative chronology

You can construct your family story as a chronology (as a linear series of biographical/family material) charting each generation and family in a logical structure beginning in the distant past and proceeding to the present. This approach is useful when the family is large and consists of numerous characters who need to be placed carefully to ensure readability.

Typically in family history you will write from the past to the present in a standard chronology. And, as noted, this is a sensible way of dealing with the large number of names, dates, events and other data collected. However, you can begin your story with a scene that is compelling; for example, a deathbed scene, a birth scene, a courtroom drama, or the details of a convict's crime – this is a technique to draw the reader in and enliven your story from the outset. Journalists call this a 'grabber lead' and you can see examples in the dramatic opening scenes of television dramas which highlight a conflict, controversy or difficult part of a person's life.

I find also that family historians now like to draw on a range of approaches including memoir, creative non-fiction and indeed fiction. It is advisable to alert the reader if you are writing fiction or introducing more imaginative elements into the story, however, as it can be confusing and indeed unethical not to do so. By the time you have finished your research on the characters and events in your family story you will be quite knowledgeable about much of it and able to draw conclusions from a variety of sources. It is a simple matter to add a phrase such as 'I think that …' or 'I imagine …' or

'It is possible …'. Some writers now choose to write in a genre such as creative non-fiction where the text becomes blurred between fiction and non-fiction. If you choose to use fiction or creative non-fiction in your story you should outline this quite explicitly in your introduction so the reader is aware of your approach from the outset.

A hook on which to hang your story

As well as a strong beginning to your story, you require a *hook* on which to hang your story. You have your dramatic opening but need other techniques to keep the reader interested. My hook when I was writing my great grandmother's story was to focus on the women in my family, a story of midwifery, and the social and economic struggles country women had to endure. By focusing on one character who lived in the same district most of her life I could incorporate much of the local history of the area as well. On your *hook*, or a string of several themes that are interconnected and which provide a coherent and useful line running through your family story, you then hang the characters, stories, generations and family events in an ordered and hopefully interesting mode.

Set up the dramatic high point at the beginning of your narrative; for example, start with the birth of an original ancestor, sketch in their childhood (or, if you do not have enough for the early years, begin with a marriage), move on to their immigration and their early years in Australia, and gradually bring the story back to that dramatic lead. This technique helps to construct a livelier story line for your reader, and frames the family story so that you can begin to insert and shape chapters, sections, stories, biographies and images for your publication. In addition, as the author *your* story is pivotal. Write about the emotional connections you have made with the characters, the events and the landmarks; why you set out on this journey; and where you are in the story.

Practical steps

As well as the creative elements of writing your family story, there are also some technical decisions you need to make about putting your story together involving computers and software. Whether you are self-publishing your book by yourself or working with a publisher, your text and images will need to be prepared and delivered in some kind of digital format.

If you are a complete beginner when it comes to computers, or would like help with the more complex tasks associated with formatting and constructing text for publishing, find and attend a relevant computer or software course before you begin your family story project. Community colleges offer such courses, and you will find computer groups and free courses at your local library. State and local genealogical societies offer their members regular meetings, free courses, and familiarisation programs on computing for family history research, recording and storing data, writing and publication. Take this book along to the classes and ask the teacher to give you the specific help you'll need to write your family history.

To use or not use Word

Opinion is divided on the use of Microsoft Word software for constructing the text of your manuscript. It is true that large files will become unstable – think of the many photographs/illustrations/maps/charts you will need to add.

However, Word continues to be the most widely used, accessible, cost-effective and convenient software for writing text. Therefore, unless you have the funds to purchase the industry-standard PageMaker <www.adobe.com/products/pagemaker/>, QuarkXPress <www.quark.com> or InDesign <www.adobe.com/products/indesign>, and are proficient in their use, stay with Word.

To limit instability in your Word files, leave complex formatting until the end of the writing and editing process, and do not insert images and other material until you are ready to print or publish. If your printer or publisher prefers images to be supplied separately, place digital files of your images and other material (clearly numbered and labelled) in separate folders and provide instructions on where the images should be placed in your text. For example, after a paragraph of text on a marriage, you would simply type <Insert Image 3.2 John and Joan's wedding> on the next line.

My strategy is to work on one chapter or section at a time, save that to a file and place it in a folder (name the files Chapter 1, Chapter 2, and so on). You can combine the chapters into the one Word document or a PDF file for your printer. Or, simply provide the printer or publisher with the individual chapter files and ask them to do it for you.

Combining files can be done in two ways:

1 *Combining Word files*. In Word 7, open your first
   file, place your cursor at the end of the text, and
   click where you want to insert the file. On the *Insert*
   tab click the arrow next to *Object* and then click
   Text from file. In the *Insert file* box locate the file
   you want, then double click on it. Continue until all
   of your files have been added into the one file.

   In older versions of Word, open your first file,
   place your cursor at the end of the text, go to the
   Formatting menu, click on *Insert* and then click on
   File. Select the next chapter to be added and click
   Insert. Continue until all of your files have been
   added into the one file.

2 *Creating a PDF file*. It is a straightforward task to
   save your combined chapters (now in the one large
   file) to PDF. If you have a recent version of Word
   (such as Word 7), go to *Save as* in your Word file
   and save to PDF. If your version of Word does not
   offer this feature, ask your printer/publisher to do
   the conversion for you.

Some family historians use Microsoft Publisher for constructing text for books. Most printers and publishers
discourage its use for manuscript or book submission,
arguing that it has reliability issues. It is still possible
to use Publisher to construct charts and maps or other
illustrations and then insert these into your text. Word
and Publisher files all convert easily to PDF format.

Look at how others write and structure their stories

Talk to your family and friends about the book and the
format you think best suits your story. Read widely.

Visit your local library, college library and/or book-shops and examine the pages of recently published memoirs, biographies, autobiographies, family histories and other non-fiction that catches your interest. Study the books that appeal most to you. Look at how the authors use language, explain their approach and structure text:

» Look at the front of each book and note if there is an ISBN number. Is there Cataloguing-in-Publication (CiP) information included? If so, how is it set out on the imprint page? (See chapter 9 for more on ISBNs and CiP.)

» Does the book have a copyright notice?

» Is there a contents page?

» Is there an index?

» Are there footnotes and/or a bibliography?

» Are the photographs placed near relevant text or collected elsewhere in the book? Do they have captions?

» How is the book structured?

» What is on the front cover? Do you like the design? Why or why not?

» Is there information on the back cover to tell the reader what the book is about?

» Quickly scan the first chapter. Would you read further? Why or why not?

Use formatting to increase readability

If you peruse published works you'll find that few are uniformly single spaced. Single spacing is useful in the front pages of your text (for example, for minor notes, the bibliography and the index.) However, for the main text use more readable spacing. In printing parlance this is termed 'leading' and you can read more on this in the Australian *Style Manual* or the *U.S. Government Style Manual* online at <www.gpoaccess.gov/stylemanual/browse.html>. Microsoft Word allows you three main spacing options, but if you decide to use a design program you will have greater choice.

Another tip for the novice self-publisher is to place page numbers in the centre at the bottom of the page thus ensuring pagination is simplified. There are complicated computations for pagination, but staying with the simple and straightforward is usually sufficient for the self-publisher at home.

Unless you have a particular liking for specific fonts, and have a good grasp of how easy or difficult various fonts are to read, stay with Times New Roman 12 pt (point size) for the main text and use one other font (in a larger point size) for headings. If you'd like to be more creative, research the pros and cons of different fonts, in particular the differences between serif and sans serif fonts. Remember, though, that many of your readers may be older and need clear and not too small type. Most self-published family history will be presented in an A4 size book. A4 facilitates a less costly production (for example, you might choose to simply photocopy a master). It is also easier for the novice self-publisher to use Word for the text, insert photographs and illustrations and display the family history effectively in A4 format.

Books and websites

For the writer of family stories questions about the past will form key shapers of the narrative and the following books and websites are excellent starting points:

Centre for Family History and Genealogy, Brigham Young University, a website on sources for writing and publishing family history <http://familyhistory.byu.edu>.

Kempthorne, Charley (1996) *For All Time: A complete guide to writing your family history,* Boynton/Cook Publishers, Heinemann, Portsmouth, NH <www.thelifestoryinstitute.com>.

KU University Writing Center, the University of Kansas <www.writing.ku.edu/~writing/guides/>.

Kyle, Noeline (2007) *Writing Family History Made Very Easy,* Allen & Unwin, Sydney <www. writingfamilyhistory.com.au>. A straightforward and practical guide to writing your family history.

Ledoux, Dennis (1993) *Turning Memories into Memoirs: A handbook for writing lifestories,* Soleil Press, Lisbon Falls, ME.

MacGibbon, John (2009) *Your Family's History: Research, write and publish it,* Ngaio Press, Wellington, NZ.

Rosier-Jones, J (2005), *Writing Your Family History: A New Zealand guide,* Random House, Auckland. An excellent text written by a popular author, see her website at <www.learntowrite.co.nz>.

Titford, John (1996) *Writing and publishing your family history,* Federation of Family History Societies, Birmingham.

Constructing chapters, creating titles

How many chapters should you include? Are they too long? Where do you place biographical information?

Can you be creative? Start with a flashback or a dramatic event? Create a title that will draw the reader in?

The answer to these questions depends on your story and where you want to take it. You can construct your family history in whatever format and genre appeals to you.

As the author it is your task to organise the biographies, stories, images and innumerable documents into a coherent, clear and readable narrative. There are several simple techniques and strategies to help you find the key themes and ideas in your story, giving you a place to start this process.

Choosing the titles for your book and chapters is an important part of the task. Titles can encapsulate key themes, comic or anecdotal phrases, family sayings, quotes from poetry or novels, descriptive words and phrases from the family story and/or family names and their source.

Constructing the book

By now, you will have written innumerable biographies of individuals and families, have an idea about your family origins, and have begun to write about places, homes, landscapes and local history. You will have learned much about the people in your past and the compelling stories that have made your journey as a researcher so interesting. You are poised at that pivotal moment of moving from the research and the first writing (or perhaps several drafts) to the construction of a manuscript that will become a book.

In *Writing Family History Made Very Easy* I write about planning, asking questions and organisation of the research material as starting points for your written text. In this chapter I want to move on to how your chapters might begin to take shape, and how their placement, design and choice of text will give your family history a general symmetry as well as a unique shape of its own.

Keep in mind that what I have to say here is very general. The histories of your ancestors will be individual and specific, and will lead you into writing and creating a manuscript that is distinctively suited to your family history. However, you can use what I say as a template, or a beginning step for collecting materials and constructing an orderly text for your book. As you work further with the text of your family history, you will discover the words, phrases, titles, chapter headings and overall thematic structure that is most suited to your publication.

Choosing a title

Most books have a title (perhaps a person's name or a quote relevant to the book's themes) and a subtitle (which can expand or amplify what the book is about). For example, you might choose to use a family name or a character's name in the title, such as Dorothy Simson did with *Caroline's Story*, to which she added the subtitle *The story of the Miskin family of Kent in Queensland*. Caroline was the author's grandmother and the family history became a journey as Simson unravelled secrets of bigamy and betrayal, family secrecy, and the strength and character of her grandmother as she coped with all of this. Or you might choose to place a character's name squarely in the main title, as Catherine Killerby did with *Ursula Frayne: A biography*. Placing the family name somewhere in the title or subtitle will add to your book's appeal and also make it easier for researchers to find it in library catalogues and bookstores.

A title as a starting point

A simple starting point for the construction of your book is to think of a title – one that will encapsulate the themes, ideas, conflicts, sorrows and joys of the family. Your title will be a reference point that you can keep returning to because it provides a focus to bring you back to a central idea or theme. It is too easy to become distracted by the large amount of data you have collected and begin to write down countless lists of events, names and dates. I have talked often to family historians about the fundamentals of writing family history, indeed any history, and I put it in these simple terms: *You do not have to write a history of everything!* Beginning with a title or indeed several titles will give you a hook or an idea to begin to shape your story. A title is shorthand for how you understand the overall story of your family history.

Did you ever have a teacher (whether at school, technical college or university) who gave you that tried-and-true advice about examination papers: to always refer back to the examination question in your answer? It is very easy to be carried away by the information you have studied or collected and end up not answering the question, instead waffling on about anything and everything. And so it is when you are writing history. Your question here is more abstract and more difficult to think about (after all, it is a complex family history), but by constructing possible titles you begin the process of reining that abstraction in.

You might have several ideas for a title, so write them down. As you write and begin to construct your book one of these titles could be your final choice, or perhaps another will emerge as more relevant and inter-esting as your story develops. Think creatively about the themes you wish to highlight; some examples are *No Man's Land* (a story about women in the family), *From Nightingale to Now* (a story about nursing) and *Dusty Diggers* (a story of men coming home from the war to battle in the outback). I have read many good titles like this which act as thematic reference points, and which also provide a starting point for writing.

Techniques and examples

Alliteration is a popular technique used in history titles, and it is an excellent device. The use of alliteration – that is, when two or more words in a phrase or sentence begin with the same sound – can catch our imagination, and the title will become part of the reader's consciousness quickly. Some examples include *Angela's Ashes*, *Mary of Maranoa*, *A Heritage Handbook*, *Grandeur and Grit: A history of Glebe*, *A People Called Pointon* and *Sons in the Saddle*.

Titles can be drawn from anywhere: from poetry, a family saying, a song or a story. For example, my mother's name was Kathleen and when she was young Dad would sing the song 'I'll take you home again, Kathleen', usually when he was a little worse with drink! My parents were divorced in the 1950s and she never spoke his name again, nor was the song sung by anyone in her hearing. When I wrote a piece for the anthology *Remembering Mothers* I called it 'I'll take you home Kathleen' a play on the words of the title of that old song. As my mother aged and became ill 'going home' took on other meanings including coming to terms with the past, remembering the good times as well as the bad – and 'home' was where we were as we cried and laughed and battled our way through the last years of her life.

The following examples of titles and subtitles show the range and scope of recent family histories. Some of the titles are short, others long. Some use language in a clever way, such as *Fifty years of Family Dollar*, while others are straightforward, such as *The McLaughlins of Tarella*. What the list reveals is that you can construct a title and subtitle in many ways, none of which is right or wrong. It is up to you to find that special theme or idea from your reading, research and final writing of the text:

Barnes, Mary Ellen (2009) *The Road to Mount Lemmon: A father, a family, and the making of Summerhaven,* University of Arizona Press, Tucson, AZ.

Dawson, Barbara (1991) *Strength in Concrete: A history of the formation and early years of the company known as AMATEK 1936–1959,* the author, Weetangera, ACT.

Fisher, Linda A & Bowers, Carrie (2009) *Agnes Lake Hickok: Queen of the circus, wife of a legend,* University of Oklahoma Press, Norman, OK.

Healy, Mary (1988) *Railways and Pastures: The Australian O'Keefes, a tribute to their pioneering efforts,* Spectrum Publications, Richmond, NSW.

Organ, Michael & Hardy, Robert (1984) *Pioneers of the Illawarra: A history of the family of Elias Organ of Wollongong, 1839–1886,* the authors, Wollongong.

Reiss, Stephen W (2009) *It Takes a Matriarch: 780 family letters from 1852 to 1888 including Civil War, farming in Illinois, life in St. Louis, life in Sacramento, life in the theater, wagon making in Davenport, and the lost family fortune,* AuthorHouse, Bloomington, IN.

Rowley, Laura (2009) *Understanding Value: Fifty years of Family Dollar,* Fenwick Publishing, Bainbridge Island, WA.

Smoker, Rod (2009) *A Humble Heritage: The*

Smoker and Stockley families and the Swan Maternity Hospital (also known as Nurse Stockley's Maternity Hospital): a brief history, R Smoker, Maylands, WA.

Warmbath, Susan (2009) *The McLaughlins of Tarella: 1890–1988*, Blue Mountains Historical Society, Wentworth Falls, NSW.

Wellesley, Jane (2009) *A Journey Through My Family: The Wellington story*, Phoenix, London.

Constructing chapters

In the same way that you can think of your book title as a focal point for your family story, each chapter title will work as an overarching statement about what is in it. You might begin with a simple list of chapters that provides a useful sequence for telling the overall family history (for example, *Origins* followed by *Leaving Ireland, The Voyage, Immigration*, and so on; or *Scottish/English/German Origins* followed by *Religious Background* then *The First Arrivals, Moving Up Country, Children, The War Years, Farmers, Moving Again*). Keep in mind that your book and chapter titles will and should change as you move further along in the writing process.

For recently arrived immigrants, the planning of chapter titles will be different. Here the emphasis is not so much on searching for overseas origins (although this can be a journey for individuals who arrived as children, perhaps as orphans and as adoptees, and who want to find out about their biological parents) but can be more an exploration of generational change, language and cultural transitions and coming to terms with both old and new family patterns. For indigenous family historians chapter headings will reflect other realities. Sally Morgan's *My Place* provides clear yet compelling chapter headings including *Triumphs and Failures, A Black Grandmother, What People are We?, Make Something of Yourself, Owning Up* and *Part of our History*. Sally Morgan has made space in her book for other voices by dividing her story into four: the first part is her story, the second is about her great uncle (*Arthur Corunna's Story*), the third is about her mother (*Gladys Corunna's Story*) and the fourth is about her grandmother (*Daisy Corunna's Story*).

A rose by any other name ...

In the commercial publishing world titles are everything – they are a brand, a promotional tool, a hook to get readers to pick up the book in the first place. Think of: *The Lord of the Rings, Sense and Sensibility, Belly Dancing for Beginners, Searching for the Secret River, The Great Gatsby, Witch and Wizard* and *Tick Tock*. These books did not sell just because of the titles, but the titles are a part of the promotional process and certainly became famous once the books were best sellers. The title of the book *The Name of the Rose* was drawn from a Latin hexameter verse, but for most of us our chapter and book names will be much less lofty.

If you are writing the story of a particular family, it is sensible to put the name of your family in the title or subtitle. It is surprising how many of us do not do this, making the book more difficult to find for a researcher browsing a catalogue or searching an online index. Including the name of the family in a title or subtitle, and possibly their place of settlement or immigration, is a sensible strategy. However, this should not prevent you from constructing a title that has a punch to it, and that is compelling and interesting. You could juxtapose opposing ideas or words in part of the title or subtitle, for example, 'reform and repression', 'demagogue or democrat', 'evil genius', 'bloody saint', 'guilt or innocence' or 'hope and despair'. These types of titles will draw your reader in.

Books and websites

The following books and websites are well worth investigating:

> Ancestry.com and Cyndislist.com have articles, websites and links to sites for writing and constructing family stories and family history. Go to their websites and search for writing, publishing, editing or formatting: <www.ancestry.com> <www.cyndislist.com>.

See also:

> Kempthorne, Charley (1996) *For All Time: A complete guide to writing your family history*, Boynton/Cook Publishers, Portsmouth, NH <www.thelifestoryinstitute.com>. Charley Kempthorne travels North America teaching and coaching writers of all ages how to write about their lives and the lives of their ancestors.
> Miller, Patti (2001) *Writing Your Life: A journey of discovery workshops & anthology*, Allen & Unwin,

Sydney <www.lifestories.com.au>. Patti Miller is a writer and teacher with a focus on memoir as a way of exploring your experience of life, other people's lives and places, topics and themes.

Robertson, Heather (1998) *Writing from Life: A guide for writing true stories,* McClelland & Stewart Inc., Toronto. Heather Robertson's focus on writing true stories debunks many myths about writing non-fiction and family 'true' stories.

4

What to put in, what to leave out

How many generations will I include in my family history?

How do I map out the generations so that readers will know how they fit within the family story?

What should I write under each name or family group?

How do I edit the biographical material families send for their entries for the family history?

How do I construct fuller accounts of women and children when I just do not have the data or if it has not survived?

How can I set limits on words, chapters, book length?

Do I have to include every name, date and event that I have collected?

These are the questions I hear from family historians who have completed their research and much of the writing. Deciding on the content to include in your chapters is a crucial part of creating a balanced, stylish and historically accurate structure for your family story.

The uneven terrain of family data

Constructing the final content of your chapters and individual biographical entries is often complicated by the large and disparate range of data you have on individual ancestors and/or families. For some family characters you will gather considerable data, for others very little. Family members may share information when asked, but this can vary from a paragraph or two to the other extreme where you receive many pages of personal and professional achievement over a long life (such as membership of organisations, sporting achievements, career/work highlights and family/personal characteristics). These fuller accounts can often be accompanied by newspaper clippings, letters, work/business papers and personal material. On the other hand, for some ancestors the detail will be sparse. This is more often the case for women and children whose lives were lived, in the past, in the less-documented domestic sphere; children's lives will barely be documented at all. There are some simple and practical strategies for dealing with this uneven terrain. You can begin by setting limits.

Setting limits

If you peruse the shelves of your local library you'll find many histories with a date/time limit. A good example of this is found in Frank Crowley's *A New History of Australia* where every chapter is mapped out by dates (1788–1810, 1810–1830, 1830–1850 and so on up to 1951–1972). Often the limits are placed in a subtitle, such as in *Women, Class and History: Feminist perspectives on Australia 1788–1978* or *These Outcast Women:*

The Parramatta Female Factory 1821–1848. Recent histories limited by date include:

> *Liberation: The bitter road to freedom, Europe 1944–1945*
>
> *1492: The year our world began*
>
> *Why Europe? The rise of the West in world history, 1500–1850*
>
> *A Bloody Picnic: Tommy's humour, 1914–1918*
>
> *The History of Australia and New Zealand from 1606 to 1890*
>
> *Just a Larger Family: Letters of Marie Williamson from the Canadian Home Front, 1940–1944*

You can also set limits through the number of generations included in the family story. When I began to write my history of the Kyle family (my father's family), I had a much bigger writing task on my hands than when I wrote about the Kirkpatricks (my mother's family). My great grandmother Mary Kirkpatrick arrived in Sydney in 1884. She had four children but only my grandfather Dave survived to adulthood. His children and grandchildren I know very well.

The Kyles (two young men) arrived in Australia in 1841. This was a very different story. I had an original ancestor who died, his widow remarried and had six more children to add to her four from the previous marriage. My great grandfather, one of the original children, had a large family and his children the same. All of the original children and their siblings, except for my great grandfather who left the family and settled elsewhere, remained in a location I knew very little about. I was very familiar with my great grandfather and his line because they settled in the same place where I was born and grew up. But the overall story was more complicated. I did not know many of the extended family who were scattered around the states of Australia.

The limits I finally set for the Kyle family history were related to time and privacy issues. I was most interested in documenting earlier generations and ensuring that this history did survive. I made a decision to end my version of this story at the fourth generation (my father's generation). For the fifth generation and since (my generation) I left a blank page at the back of the book for individuals to put in their own family lineage, stories and generational connections and comments.

For some family historians there is a real desire to map the story and include all of the generations to the present day, including the stories of still living children and grandchildren. I was not prepared to do this because, although I know many of the stories of my first cousins and their families, I thought it unnecessary to include such recent detail. There was a time when family historians published long lists of names, dates and personal family data in their books. With the arrival of the Internet and the ease with which genealogical information can know be published online, privacy issues have been raised; however, the practice of uploading personal data about families has continued. Further comment on privacy is provided in chapter 9, and up-to-date discussion on the privacy issues relative to genealogy and publication can be found on the following websites:

Cregan Ancestry Privacy Issues <http://homepages. rootsweb.ancestry.com/~cregan/privacy.htm>
Identity Theft <www.identitytheft.org>

Privacy Survival Guide
<www.privacyrights.org/FS/fs1-surv.htm>
Who Owns Genealogy? Cousins and Copyright
<www.genealogy.com/genealogy/14_cpyrt.html>

Step 1: What to put in

If you would like to ensure your family story achieves symmetry and balance, make every effort to give each individual (man, woman and child) a balanced and fair description. This is an important consideration when planning your text. The following information categories can help to ensure your entries are balanced and fair.

Births, deaths, marriages

Although you generally need to purchase the birth, death or marriage certificates of early ancestors (as these provide useful information on characters you know little about), you may sometimes find enough information for some biographical entries in the various birth, marriage and death indexes. It is up to you, as the family historian, to decide which full certificates are required.

It is also the case that for the first arrivals to a country, state or county, births of children are often the only avenue you have of tracking these ancestors. The birth certificate can tell us much: perhaps about a place of living, about the church used for the baptism, and certainly will indicate the name of the informant. The interstate and intrastate movement of these early families may be surprising (why did they go to that place?), and other family information (occupation of the father, for example) will be provided. Ages, dates and family relationships can also be checked. For each character included in your family history, their birth, marriage and death details are the frame for how you then begin to write the entry.

Parentage

On the marriage certificate you will normally find the parentage details of both groom and bride and these should be listed where possible. Try to include the parentage and other details of the person marrying into the family. Also, women's parentage is sometimes omitted from information sent to you by relatives or others. As the family historian it is your task to do some follow-up research to obtain the relevant data to complete entries more fully.

Work

Try to list the occupations of both bride and groom before and after their marriage. Too often you will find only the occupation of males listed. However, if you take the time to contact relatives, especially the children and/ or grandchildren, you'll find that many women worked before marriage and certainly were part of the family business (on farms or in town) after marriage. Look at general books on occupations and on women's work to provide greater depth and context for your entries. Here are two examples:

Daly, Mary E (1997) *Women and Work in Ireland,* Dundalgan Press, Louth, Ireland.

Ward, Margaret (2008) *Female Occupation: Women's employment 1850–1950,* Countryside Books, Newbury, UK.

Schooling

Most children had an experience of formal or informal schooling. If they did not go to school – as happened often with girls who were kept home to help with domestic work, indigenous children and children in very remote areas – this too affected their childhood experience and is part of their story.

On all of my entries I have tried to fill in when and where individuals went to school. For some entries I had the actual information from school records, at other times their religion (say Catholic), or I had oral histories that gave me insights about their schooling. At other times I contacted the family to find out more information.

The other woman

When a man marries into a family, you will know his full name – after all, his surname is the family name. This is rarely the case for women. Often you will not have the maiden or previous name, so this is an excellent time to do the additional research to find out. I telephoned family and did as much extra research as possible in an effort to fill in these blanks. Knowing when and where 'Joan' (all I might have) was born, her parents' names and what she did before she married did make the entries richer and more readable. These books may be of assistance as you construct biographies of women in your ancestral past:

De Bartolo Carmack, Sharon (1998) *A Genealogist's Guide to Discovering Your Female Ancestors*, Betterway Books, Cincinnati, OH.

Kyle, Noeline (1988) *We Should've Listened to Grandma: Women and family history*, Allen & Unwin, Sydney.

Other details

Other details that might be listed in entries are the musical, sporting and community interests of each person. For example, try to detail the relationship between family members such as sisters, brothers and/or aunts, uncles and cousins. Life was lived in much smaller circles pre-1950, especially in country areas, and families were close and spent their work and leisure time as a family group more often than happens today.

Step 2: What to leave out

Deciding what *not* to put in is very important. Here are some guidelines:

Editing biographies

It might be constructive for you, as the writer and editor of the family story, to provide some sort of correspondence in the length, content and placing of your biographical entries. If you receive lengthy details from family members about their ancestors, it is often the case that these will need significant editing and trimming for inclusion.

Length

When planning the entries for my Kyle family history I found that I wanted to construct lengthy biographical or thematic stories for original ancestors, first arrivals and second generations. It seemed to me that the research I was doing into immigration records, in newspapers, in births, deaths and marriage records, with oral history and with other sources was establishing a practical base, a record of material and history for that more distant past. I believed that these early ancestors were entitled to a longer more complex entry than I would write for more recent ancestors. These lives were lived in the distant past and would be soon obliterated by time. It was up to me to make sure they were recorded in substantive detail, and with accuracy and flair.

However, as I moved into the third and fourth generations the entries were smaller. This was a logical progression: depending on how many children were born, the number of individual families, children and grandchildren grew and therefore the biographies could not be as detailed as earlier entries.

As a general rule, collecting additional details from family members is useful, but the reader can be bored very easily by a long list of local associations, a character's special preferences for travel, community events and/or family events. It is your job to edit your biographical entries carefully so that each entry is reasonably balanced, while still retaining the unique flavour of each character.

When I looked at the structure of the Kyle family history, I found that I wanted to write at least a few pages on my early biographical entries. I spent more time perusing newspapers and pestered family members for additional information to make sure the original ancestors and first arrivals were well documented. For later entries, I tried to keep to a half-page for each one. To some extent this was related to cost because with a large number of entries for children and grandchildren the size of the book was growing. I had already discussed book length with my printer and knew roughly how many pages overall I could run to. With some entries, of course, a few lines was all I could manage. This was especially the case for children and grandchildren who died at birth or shortly thereafter, or individuals I had very little information on despite my best efforts to find it.

Controversial subject matter

One of the often-asked questions in family history relates to family secrets. There is considerable debate among family historians on the ethics of using controversial subject matter in your stories, and I write further on this topic in chapter 9. I grew up in the 1940s and 1950s, an era when children were not told the 'truth' about their family or individual circumstances, and many of my cousins and friends from that era found out about painful events related to their own lives when they were older. This was one of the reasons I decided to limit the number of generations in my Kyle family history. In addition, older members of the family have very different perceptions of events in the past.

Younger members of the family might look back at personal issues of bigamy, separation or divorce, illegitimacy, adoption, criminality, family discord, bankruptcy and other family conflict with equanimity. Your elderly aunts and uncles, grandparents and indeed your own parents may not. There may be extended family members you do not know who can also be hurt or offended by indiscriminate disclosure of such things. It is therefore of utmost importance that you inform people of your intention to publish and ask their permission to do so. Be sensitive and do not use information that will hurt or offend living people. Be aware there are legal and privacy issues; I write further on these in chapter 9.

When discussing family secrets with family historians I am often told 'But it's the truth!', or 'But it's such a good story!'. The 'truth' is relative, however; if you talk to a range of people associated with any event, each one will have their own version of it. Perhaps the most controversial subjects in family history are adoption, domestic violence and the sexual abuse of children. If the publication of controversial material about family members living today or in the distant past will hurt or be derogatory – or, worse, is false or unable to be proved – it is irresponsible, unethical and immoral to publish it.

Books and websites

The following books are useful models for constructing family stories and provide a variety of structures to study for building a family story:

> Forster, Margaret (2000) *The Memory Box*, Penguin Books, London. This acclaimed family memoir takes the reader across three generations to challenge assumptions about family life.
> Kyle, Noeline (2008) *Music, Myth & Memory: A Kyle family history* (with Joyce Lawson), e-book edition, further details from <www. writingfamilyhistory.com.au>. My second family history is written as a simple chronology with biographical entries and an overarching theme of

traditional Irish fiddle music brought to Australia
by my ancestors and passed down through
children and grandchildren to today.

O'Faolain, Nuala (1996) *Are You Somebody?*
Sceptre Books, London. Nuala O'Faolain writes
a remarkable memoir about a 1950s childhood
where she was raised by an alcoholic mother and a
charming, feckless and mostly absent father.

Trubshaw, Bob (2005) *How to Write & Publish
Local & Family History Successfully,* Heart of
Albion Press, Wymeswold, UK, further details
from <www.hoap.co.uk>. This excellent source
book has up-to-date information and advice on
how to write and publish family history. The
book includes technical but easy-to-access sources
and advice on the latest technology including
e-publishing, e-books and digital photography.

5

Making sense

Once you have determined how to shape chapters, titles, biographies and stories it is time to look more closely at your text and edit for sense, clarity, accuracy and readability.

Continue to ask yourself questions. Why are you writing this family story and what do you want to see in the final manuscript?

Remember: write early, write quickly. However, revise slowly to polish grammar and punctuation and to examine voice and tone. Ensure that the writing is natural, not stilted. Check for overstatement. Take out fancy words.

Try different options for words and phrases. Put your manuscript in a drawer for a week or longer before you look at it again.

Only after you have revised your work thoroughly should you show it to anyone else.

There is good advice on editing to be found in your local bookshop, library and on the Internet.

Staying on track

Part of the revision and editing task is to ensure that your paragraphs, pages and chapters make sense, flow easily and help readers follow your story. To help keep you on track as you write, draw up a document that displays the structure of your family history generation by generation, family by family, and then lists individuals under each generation and family. Refer to the document regularly as you write and edit. Checking language use and paragraph placement will ensure your family history is not a confusing trek through too many disparate and unconnected events, people and histories.

Look at editing and grammar texts to help with writing and revision. A great many up-to-date and well-written guides to editing, punctuation and grammar, and how to revise and edit writing, have been published worldwide in recent years. Check local, state and national libraries in your district or state for available texts. Search databases and catalogues for words and phrases such as *editing, writing, editing history, editing family history, referencing genealogy, grammar, style manual, student guides to writing.* Keep a dictionary and thesaurus open on your desk or check online versions. These are your best sources for word and language checking. Websites that focus on writing, editing and revising your work are also useful and readily found.

Books

This list of books will get you started on your editing task:

Argante, Jenny (2004) *Constructive Editing*, Hen
  Enterprises, Tauranga, New Zealand.

The Chicago Manual of Style (2010) The University
  of Chicago Press, 16th edition, Chicago/London.

Curthoys, Ann & McGrath, Ann (2009) *How to
  Write History That People Want to Read*, UNSW
  Press, Sydney.

Hughes, Janet & Wallace, Derek (2010) *Fit to Print:
  The writing and editing style guide for Aotearoa
  New Zealand*, Dunmore Publications, Wellington,
  New Zealand.

Kaplan, Bruce (2008) *Editing Made Easy*, Penguin
  Books, Melbourne/London.

Kelleher Storey, William (1999) *Writing History: A
  guide for students*, Oxford University Press, New
  York/Oxford.

Kleu, Tony (2006) *Writing Good English: A concise
  guide to keeping it simple and getting it right*, John
  Fairfax Publications, Sydney.

Ross-Larson, Bruce (1996) *Edit Yourself: A manual
  for everyone who works with words*, W. W.
  Norton & Company, New York/London.

Tredinnick, Mark (2006) *The Little Red Writing
  Book*, UNSW Press, Sydney.

Tremewan, Tanya & Daphne Brasell Associates
  (1997) *Write, Edit, Print: Style manual for
  Aotearoa New Zealand*, AGPS Press with Lincoln
  University Press, Canberra, ACT.

Venolia, Jan (1997) *Write Right! A desktop digest of
  punctuation, grammar and style*, Ten Speed Press/
  Periwinkle Press, Berkeley, CA.

Online dictionaries

These days there are many good, free dictionaries available online. Here is just one: <www.yourdictionary. com>. The full text of other dictionaries, including *The Macquarie Dictionary* <www.macquariedictionary.com. au>, are available online for a fee.

Checking facts

Revision of text will require you to check facts: place names, family names, buildings, organisations, events, unfamiliar overseas data, rivers, dates, simple typos. The list is long. If you have constructed a *style sheet* you will be well on your way, but invariably there will be unusual or difficult words, phrases or names that can lead to errors and typos.

You can ask a family member, friend and/or fellow writer/historian to read your manuscript for factual errors. But it is likely that as the author of the text you will be best placed to do an initial check of the facts. You have spent many months, perhaps years, gathering research data and linking new facts to your established data. You are the expert.

One strategy used by both beginning and experienced writers is to put the completed draft manuscript in a drawer for a few weeks or a month or two. When you go back to it you will read it with a fresh eye and be able to see factual errors more easily.

Repetition and consistency

Family historians must contend with much overlapping and interrelated family information that is relevant to many families and individuals. It is therefore easy to repeat stories and events. Repetitive text and inconsistent use of language, style, spelling and structural elements are the constant bugbears of family stories. As the writer of the text it is also difficult to see repetition because you tend to become enmeshed in the writing and do not readily see errors or repeated text. Asking someone to read your draft manuscript will pick up some repetition and inconsistency. As with fact checking, you will need a range of strategies including putting the manuscript away and coming back to it some weeks later.

Adding content

Editing is not just about cutting text. It also involves adding in and shaping the story more fully, and adding flair, colour and emotion.

Some of your paragraphs or chapters will be too short. Expand on the central idea, or it might be more appropriate to reposition the text elsewhere. Use judicious research to help expand your topics. You can add colour and texture to your writing by adding more detail to your descriptions of houses, land, people, churches, landscape. To flesh out characters, look at their place in the family (eldest or youngest, tall or short, events surrounding growing up) to write more fully about them.

Anecdotes and remembered conversations which relate directly to your writing themes and characters can add depth and colour. Add in your personal reflections on the subject matter. As the researcher and writer of the family story you will have gained considerable insight into the family and its many characters, events and stories. Including your reflections and making judicious comment from time to time will enrich the text.

In my workshops and books I have provided examples of how you can add to your family story by incorporating previously published stories, descriptions and ideas, especially those larger stories from local, national and internationally published books. In these and many other works you will find stories about places, characters, and local and world events that are useful for your writing. Remember, though, to cite your sources and check any copyright restrictions that might apply (see below and chapter 9). You can also use your imagination. You can imagine, interpret and assume from your facts and from your family stories. But don't think you have to rewrite the history of everything. What you can do is add in and incorporate relevant description and ideas that are interesting and useful to your family story.

It is much harder to write evocatively about the ancient past and characters who lived long ago. We know only the bare details of these ancestors' births, marriages and deaths. However, this does not mean writing about them should be barren and dull. Here is an example from the story of my great grandmother Nurse Mary Kirkpatrick (Noeline Kyle [2001] *Memories & Dreams: A biography of Nurse Mary Kirkpatrick*, the author, Mullumbimby, NSW). I knew that Mary Kirkpatrick had nursed her dying daughter for two weeks just before Christmas 1882 because this is on the death certificate. I knew it must have been cold as it was winter in Belfast. But that is all I knew. It was enough, however, to write the following:

> Mary Kirkpatrick had sat beside the bed for two weeks bathing her daughter Janet's tiny feverish body in warm water and feeding her sips of warm broth and milk.
>
> She bathed the secretions from her eyes and nose and gently rubbed the child's hot forehead with a cold compress.
>
> Mary knew about illness and death as she had seen her own friend's children slip away like this. She had read about childhood illnesses and medicine as she had an interest in the field. She knew too much to think her daughter would survive but not enough to save her.

I could say that my great grandmother responded in certain ways because by the time I had finished my research I knew something about why and how and in what way she went about her life. There is always a modicum of probability in the writing of history and a great deal of uncertainty for the historian as you map out a way through the myths and the milestones of these past lives. However, with some imagination, interpretation and the help of other written stories you can construct livelier and historically compelling family stories.

Revision

Effective and readable text is short, sharp, concise and clear. When sentences are more than twenty words in length they become imprecise, and are often abstract and obscure. When rereading your pages try to eliminate overly long sentences. It is a simple matter to cut sentences into smaller bites, and rewrite and sharpen what it is you are trying to communicate.

Conversely, short sentences are not nearly enough on their own. Vary the length of sentences and maintain a balance throughout your text. Look at Jonathan Franzen's *The Corrections* where sentences are sometimes so long they fill a page. However, Franzen also uses short sentences, witty dialogue and sharp, short phrases which work to snap the reader back to attention. If one word will do the work of two or three, use it instead. Check your writing against your original title, chapter headings and subheadings. Shift stories, characters and ideas that are better placed elsewhere.

Books and online resources to help with revision

Begin with these websites:

Epton, Kim (2007) *Get it Write!* Hesperian Press, Carlisle, WA, online at <www.hesperianpress. com>. This is a free downloadable PDF booklet with editing, revision, grammar and word usage advice for the writer and self-publisher.

Gilks, Marg (2001) *Grammar Gaffes and How to Avoid Them*, <www.writing-world.com/basics/ gaffes.shtml>. Marg Gilks is a proofreader and freelance copy editor and she has further advice on her website <www.scripta-word-services.com>.

Strunk, William Jr, *The Elements of Style,* online

at <www.crockford.com/wrrrld/style.html>.
Strunk's excellent book can be found in many
libraries and is downloadable from many sites
including this one.

Editing references/bibliography/ footnotes

Check the consistency of your referencing and ensure
the contents page, headings and page numbers match the
body of the work. Have you used the same style for captions and the layout of photographs, maps and charts?
Acknowledge all sources and resources including phone
conversations, oral histories, emailed information and
downloaded data from the Internet. You have collected
innumerable names, dates and other facts from books,
libraries, newspapers, articles, bulletins, registers, directories, almanacs, bibliographies, biographical dictionar-
ies, online indexes, friends, family members and more.
All need careful checking and acknowledgment. As
Richard Lackey notes in his work (see below), it is not
acceptable to acknowledge your sources as follows:
'Reference material collected by my friend'
'My cousin's books'
'A death certificate'
'File #6284'
'A roll of microfilm sold by the government'
For useful guidance on checking sources and references
for your book see:
Lackey, Richard S (1980) *Cite Your Sources:
A manual for documenting family histories
and genealogical records*, University Press of

Mississippi, Jackson, MS.

Shown Mill, Elizabeth (1997) *Evidence? Citation & analysis for the family historian*, Genealogical Pub. Co., Baltimore, MD.

Shown Mill, Elizabeth (2009) *Evidence Explained: Citing history sources from artifacts to cyberspace*, Genealogical Pub. Co., Baltimore, MD.

Editing the text

Once you have put your writing away for a few weeks or a month, and have completed initial revision and checking, it is time for a *major revision* of your family story. Read your text as though you are completely new to it. Do you have a hook on which to hang your story? Are there coherent themes and ideas? If not, are there themes that are more compelling, perhaps some that you want to cut out? Keep in mind that a family story is not drawn from every document you have collected. Your family story is a narrative drawing on central themes, stories and ideas to bring family, characters and events to life.

Writing non-fiction is as much an artistic endeavour as is writing fiction. The rhythm and tone of the language is important – your reader will want to find flair, interest, hope and joy and it is your task to inject the writing with compassion, conflict, sensitivity, elegance, optimism and the range of human emotion you expect to find within a family. At the same time your writing should be crisp, clear and easily read. Take the time to edit, revise and add to ensure your story is well told and presented professionally.

A structural edit

A structural edit is a major revision to consider the manuscript's overall coherence. This is where you consider if some chapters would work better if moved elsewhere; maybe some are too long and wordy, others too short.

Do you have enough information to complete your chapters? Are there gaps you would like to fill with more research? Your aim is to ensure the family story reads well, has coherent themes and works as a well-structured piece of text.

Examine the basic story line, how it works, whether the structure (chapters, characters, events, sections, overall story line) fit what you set out to do. Look at repetition (of ideas, words and paragraphs) and inconsistencies, and look for grammatical errors and typos (although you may not be specifically looking for these).

A copy edit

Copy editing is sometimes referred to as line editing. One way to do this yourself is to print out your text and work systematically, line by line, looking for errors of word usage, sentence structure, misspellings and grammar. If you are able to pay a professional copy editor to do this for you, they will also check for sense, clarity, and grammatical and mechanical accuracy.

Check for visual as well as language consistency. For example, are type, headings, captions and pagination consistent? Do they suit/support the page layout and story structure?

Professional editors and other resources

Try these websites if you are looking for editorial guidance or assistance:

Abbreviations.com <www.abbreviations.com>
American Copy Editors Society
  <www.copydesk.org>
Bartleby.com, Great Books Online
  <www.bartleby.com>
Editorial Freelancers Association <www.the-efa.org>
Institute of Professional Editors (provides links to
  the societies of editors in each Australian state and
  territory) <www.iped-editors.org>
The New Zealand Society of Authors
  <www.authors.org.nz/wawcs0139327/writers_
  toolkit.html>
Refdesk.com (for checking current and unusual
  facts) <www.refdesk.com/welcome.html>
Society of Editors and Proofreaders (UK)
  <www.sfep.org.uk>
Wikipedia's editing, proofreading and copy editing
  links and information, for example
  <http://en.wikipedia.org/wiki/Proofreading>

Checklist for editing

You can find checklists for editing both online and in editing books. The following list is a truncated version to get you started on the task:

1   Check each word, phrase, sentence and paragraph/
    section.
2   Check spelling, hyphens, capital letters, numbers,
    names, places and terms against a style sheet.

3 Examine and correct overly long sentences and awkward writing.

4 Delete words, phrases, paragraphs that are unnecessary.

5 Take out vague words and woolly phrases (*actually, undoubtedly, at this point in time*).

6 Take out unnecessary words and phrases (*the fact that, take into consideration, in the event that*).

7 Remove clichés and fashionable words and phrases (*ongoing, scenario, grassroots*).

8 Look for 'stating the obvious' errors (*abolish altogether, grateful thanks, I myself, pre-planned*)

9 Check for overstatement (*colossal, terrific, massive, mighty, wonderful*).

10 Check for overused words ('very' as in *very tired, very happy, very unhappy*).

11 Watch tautology (*link together, follow after, descend downwards, wealthy millionaire, historical forebear*).

12 Read your text out as though to an audience. This will help to identify poor placement of commas and awkward sentence structure.

Family history templates

A template is a guide – a pattern or model that you can follow, study, take ideas from and build on to create a family story of your own.

I have already noted that it is a good strategy to look at how other writers publish their family stories. I have said that focusing on a character might lead to using a biographical frame for your story. This is just one way of writing and publishing the family story. In addition, a template might be found in the use of chronology, local history, oral history, occupational themes, immigration, convict history, economic or political themes, memoir, autobiography or fiction.

The following chapter template and basic sample family story are brief examples of how a family history can be written and presented. Of course, there are myriad ways to structure a family history story and you will find the right one for you.

Chapter templates

Following is just one suggested way of organising your chapters.

Origins

For non-indigenous North Americans, Australians and New Zealanders, countries of origin can be as widespread as Scotland, Ireland, Wales, England, Italy or Germany. You may also find Chinese, Greek, South-East Asian, Spanish, Indian, African and Portuguese ancestors; in fact, origins will often be a mix of several countries, many religions and diverse socioeconomic and political backgrounds. For indigenous peoples and recently arrived immigrants and refugees, origins are a complex story involving different cultures and countries as diverse as China, the Phillipines, Vietnam, Somalia, Sudan, Afghanistan, Iraq, Lebanon, the Pacific Islands, and many more.

In a chapter about a family's origins, do not think you have to write everything (that is, rewrite the history of the world, of Scotland, of Ireland, of Germany or Africa) but instead try to focus on what is relevant for your ancestors. Certainly include all of the historical data you have available such as parentage, where individuals were born, occupations, grandparents and/ or other ancestors, general socioeconomic conditions, religion, schooling and other local historical contexts. However, keep within the bounds of your family's geographical, social, political and economic contexts and use the specific historical information that highlights their life experiences and which begins the shaping of the family narrative in a coherent and unique way. Here are some specific suggestions on what to include:

» Include the birth information of your first arrivals to the new country and their genealogy as far as it can be ascertained. However, if the genealogy (names/dates) is long and complicated it might be better placed in an appendix for reference.

» Discuss religion/spiritual ancestry and where it began.

» Record where and when parents and grandparents married.

» Offer some description of places.

» Include local history and background material on places, family, individuals and communities.

» Provide information on the socioeconomic conditions of your ancestors. Were they poor farmers or rich merchants? Were they soldiers, sailors, adventurers or convicts? Were they miners, shopkeepers, doctors or midwives? Occupations, education, social position and economic circumstance provide much of the colour, contrast and complexity you can use to map out your ancestor's original lives.

» Detail the lives of women, including the work they did before marriage and later in the home.

» For ancestors who immigrated, describe how they travelled to and joined their ship for the journey.

» Build a picture of your ancestors' childhood. Were they the first-born, the youngest, an only child, one of many children? Did they go to school? Were they working at any early age? Can you imagine/describe physical characteristics such as hair colour, eye colour, height? Were they happy/sad, outgoing/reserved?

» Write about characters' relationships with siblings, parents, friends and cousins. What was each one's age and place in family? Describe these and other characteristics at different times in the history cycle.

Immigration

Writing a chapter on immigration is a mixture of writing about leaving a place of origin – that is, the journey – and arrival in a new country.

Begin your story with the ship:

» How did you find the immigration record?
» Were you surprised by some of the details?
» Was there a problem with the spelling of names?
» How did you solve these problems?

You may find more specific information at:

Log of Logs by Ian Nicholson <http://freepages. genealogy.rootsweb.ancestry.com/~nzbound/logs. htm>

Cyndi's List – Ships & Passenger Lists at <www.cyndislist.com/ships.htm>

Next, investigate the voyage. Do you have details of the voyage, such as a diary or the surgeon's report? The National Archives (UK) have a webpage with Royal Naval Medical Officers' journals from 1793 to 1880; these can be downloaded and searched at: <www.nationalarchives.gov.uk/surgeonsatsea/>.

Were your ancestors assisted/unassisted immigrants, convicts or free passengers? See sources of information at:

Ellis Island <www.cyndislist.com/ellis.htm>.

Cyndi's List is an ever-expanding website

providing information on every topic imaginable. This Ellis Island site is invaluable, listing everything from publications, passenger records, Ellis Island records, photographic records and online databases.

The National Archives (UK) <www.nationalarchives.gov.uk/nra/>. The National Archives are the starting point for your research and finding information on emigration. Go to *Records > In-depth research guides* and click on *Emigration.*

Public Record Office of Northern Ireland (PRONI) <www.proni.gov.uk>. PRONI have a page on family history with a range of information and online indexes. Their local history leaflets include an emigration series with information on the United States, Canada and Australia.

Now look at your ancestors' arrival and life in their new country:

» Who sponsored your ancestors? Was it a relative, a local landowner or merchant or a professional immigration agent?

» Did your ancestors settle permanently in their port of destination? Where were they living?

» Were there births, marriages and deaths during this time period?

» Did the family leave their port of destination for a country area, another state, another town or city? If so, why?

The first arrivals

Your first arrivals into a new country, county, state or place are a link to the past (place of origin) and are also a writing pathway to recording their new life. Here's some suggestions for what to include in this chapter:

» At some point after arrival in a new country, most young men and women will marry and then settle in a location to establish a family. Some will move further interstate or establish themselves in another district where there is work or prospects of farming. Begin your writing with this marriage.

» Add the parentage of the wife or husband of your ancestor.

» Describe/outline where your ancestor was born, their age on arrival, occupation/s, any physical characteristics (from a photograph or immigration records), and any other personal details.

» Describe the church, witnesses to the marriage and place of marriage. What season was it? Could they sign their names or did they use a cross? Look at local and major newspapers and find the day/year of the marriage (or other event such as a birth). Take a news items and write about the marriage in relation to it. Margaret Forster, in her book *Hidden Lives: A family memoir*, begins her story with the birth of her grandmother during a cold, bitter winter:

Boxing Day 1869. A Sunday. Snow lay thick on the ground, thick on the cathedral roof, thick on stout castle ramparts ... [she goes on to write about weeks of bitter weather and the white silence of the streets and then about the birth] ... In a house in one of these turnings, John Street, a young woman, nineteen years old, was giving birth to her first child. The woman's name was Annie Jordan. She called her baby Margaret Ann. Three months later she had her daughter baptized in the church of St Mary. Not quite two years after that Annie Jordan died, aged twenty-one, leaving Margaret Ann an orphan ...

» What area or region did the first generation after the marriage or arrival settle?
» Include information on the socioeconomic context if you can. For example, what was the climate like (was there a drought, floods, good times/bad times) during the arrival/settlement years?
» Describe the indigenous history and background to the place and times.
» Detail the lives of women and children, including details of domestic work and outside/paid work. Local history books can help to fill in general detail if specifics are not known.
» Investigate the working life of your male ancestors. For example, if farmers, were they growing crops, and if so, what were these crops? Were they running cattle or keeping pigs? Did the men in the family have to clear land (check local histories for general detail)? Did the men work off the farm to make ends meet?
» Include the births of children, marriages, separations and any deaths.

The generations

For this chapter, begin with a simple chronology. After the first arrivals, your next chapter might be the children of the first arrivals. You might then add another arrival with their children/grandchildren. You could also have children/grandchildren in differing locations, with differing occupations and/or interests. All of these diverse lives and events can provide entry points for your writing.

Sample chapter for a family history family story

Following is a template for one generation and their descendants. It is a relatively brief example, but it demonstrates how each entry should have reader appeal with a simple narrative format outlining the biographies, events and stories of each generation.

To give you some background, this story is one of sixteen chapters in my history of the Kyle family *Music, Myth & Memory*. William Kyle was one of five children born to Henry Kyle who hailed from Roscommon, Ireland. Henry died young and his widow Esther remarried and with her new husband and now large brood of children moved to Murwillumbah in New South Wales. Henry and Esther's children – Thomas, William, Mary Ann and Eliza Agnes – remained in Murwillumbah and many descendants live there today. My great great grandfather and the youngest child Henry left the Tweed Valley and settled on the Macleay River. I could write with some knowledge about my own family along the Macleay River, but had to work hard at the biographies and stories of other family because these were new stories to me. William Kyle's entry and those of his children illustrate how adding in some extra detail (for example, on his wife Elizabeth's incarceration at Kenmore Mental Hospital, his son's war record and the broader battles around him of that terrible war, and the poignancy of William's plea to the rather heartless Defence Department for information on his son's grave) provides a richer story. I had considerable help from extended family who sent me stories and answered my additional queries with generosity and patience.

William Kyle 1849-1931

William Kyle was born on 25 December 1849 at Bendolba on the Williams River and baptised in St. Joseph's Catholic Parish, East Maitland on 29 January 1850. William was eighteen when he rode the almost 700 kilometres with his brother William from Dungog to the Tweed Valley in 1868. The brothers were excellent horsemen, however, and would have made good time stopping only to camp and find fresh food along the way. Thomas' son Thomas Alfred was a renowned lightweight jockey with the Victor Foy stable and rode many winners in Sydney and Melbourne. There are surviving stories of the wild Kyle brothers riding their horses through the streets of Murwillumbah.

When he arrived in the Tweed Valley, William worked initially sawing timber for Messrs Hall and Alfred Boardman. He took out a conditional purchase of 90 acres in 1882 at Dungay Creek but forfeited the land in May 1890. Conditional purchases were normally forfeited due to inability to pay the balance of the purchase price over three years. It was not difficult however to arrange longer terms for payment thus it is unusual for forfeiture to take place at this time.[1] Perhaps William preferred some other arrangement. In any case he began dairying at Tygalgah, a farming district near Murwillumbah, in 1890 and remained there until his death.

William married Elizabeth McCarthy on 16 November 1884 in St. Francis' Catholic Church, Murwillumbah. Witnesses to the marriage were his brother Thomas

William Kyle.
SOURCE Courtesy of the Tweed River Regional Museum

and half sister Ellen Neylan. Elizabeth McCarthy was born in Ireland in 1854 and died on 31 August 1921 at Kenmore Mental Hospital near Goulburn. She was buried on 3 September 1921 in the Kenmore Mental Hospital Cemetery. Elizabeth was admitted to Kenmore Mental Hospital on 17 April 1907; she was 47 years of age. Kenmore Estate, Goulburn, had been appointed as a Hospital for the Insane in July 1894 and is now closed. The burial ground was a paddock next to the hospital and there are no markings or headstones for any graves. There are no records to show why Elizabeth was admitted to this asylum, but historical works on women in mental hospitals report that their incarceration could be for simple depression as well as for more serious psychotic episodes.[2] Married women, in particular, had few rights and their capacity to maintain their own sense of self and happiness depended very much on the benevolence and generosity of a husband. Once admitted to the asylum, Elizabeth remained until her death fifteen years later in 1921. Why and in what circumstances that decision was made remains a mystery yet to be solved.

The death of William's only son during WW1 was a terrible blow. His son was killed in May 1917 at a time when William must have been suffering also from the difficulties associated with his wife's illness. The letters from William to the Defence Department reveal his anguish at not knowing exactly what had happened to his son and the despair of the finality of it all. On 11 March 1918, William wrote to the department about his son's war pension:

... If you could let me know what engagement he got wounded in it is hard [to] bare [*sic*] he been [*sic*] the

> only boy the flower of the flock cut of [*sic*] in the
> prime of life he was my only hope it was that Dearly
> beloved boy I was looking forward for help later on
> and now on the verg [*sic*] of sixty and no other to
> take his place ...

After some further intervention by his daughter Elizabeth (Lizzie), William was granted a pension from 19 July 1917 of 35/- as the next of kin. In May 1922 William wrote again to the department on the matter of his son's grave and its headstone:

> I understand it was to be only a temprey [*sic*] one
> that the first head stone was to be erected. If
> they are completed with this panel head stone I
> will have [unclear] ... but if they replace the ones
> [unclear] I dont want them. Dear Sir you say those
> copys [*sic*] will be sent poast [*sic*] free. I fail to see
> how this are coming poast free for six copies. I have
> to send 3 shillings worth of stamps but I want to
> know if they are finished. He gave his life for his
> country and his freedom and [being] the only son I
> think I am entitled to a little more than a copy of
> his grave.

William received a pompous reply from the department pointing out some discrepancy in his understanding of the processes involved in obtaining photographs of his son's grave and the progress of same. Scant recognition one would think, of the sacrifice of his son's life and none, of course, for his own grief and despair. William died on 4 July 1931 at Murwillumbah.

The children of William Kyle and Elizabeth McCarthy

William Henry Kyle, 1889–1917

William Henry, known as Henry, was the only son of William Kyle and Elizabeth McCarthy. He was born in 1889 at Tygalgah. Henry was educated at a public school and at St. Patrick's Convent, Murwillumbah. He was a labourer and living at 181 Bourke Street, Sydney, when he enlisted for war service on 2 March 1916 in the 17th Battalion. As Henry boarded the troop ship *Euripides* on 9 September 1916 he celebrated his 25th birthday. He had brown eyes, dark hair and was short and stocky. It was to be a brief period of service. He disembarked at Plymouth on 26 October 1916 and proceeded on the *Golden Eagle* to France on 13 December 1916. Five months later in the terrible and now infamous battle at Bullecourt, Somme, France, he was fatally wounded. Henry was transported

to the General Hospital, Rouen, where he died on 2 May 1917. He was buried at 146 Sever Cemetery, Rouen, France. More than 7,000 Australian soldiers died between 3 May and 17 May 1917 in this one British Army offensive alone. A terrible cost.[3]

William Henry Kyle.
SOURCE Joyce Lawson

L–R: William Henry Kyle, Henry Lockwood, John Strang Drylie.
SOURCE Joyce Lawson

Elizabeth (Lizzie) Kyle 1885–1966

Lizzie Vickerman.
SOURCE Sharon Collier

Lizzie was born 18 September 1885 at Tygalgah. She married Albert Holm Vickerman in 1919 at Drummoyne, Sydney. He was a widower. Albert's previous wife was Ada Beatrice Hart and he was the father of two sons and two daughters. Albert died in 1925 at Newtown, Sydney. Lizzie died on 31 August 1966 at Redcliffe, a northern suburb of Brisbane. She is buried in the Catholic Section of the General Cemetery at Redcliffe.

The children of Lizzie Kyle and Albert Holm Vickerman

Catherine (Katie) Vickerman, 1887–c. 1893

Catherine was born in 1887 at Tygalgah and died when she was about six years of age in Murwillumbah. There are no records of her death or burial.

Winifred Noeleen Vickerman 1924–2002

Winifred Noeleen Vickerman, known as Win, was born on 22 January 1924 in Sydney. Win's father died when she was twelve months old. She grew up at Five Dock and attended All Hallows School, Haberfield, and then Domremy College at Five Dock. After leaving school Win worked in retail in Toowoomba, Queensland, and within an advertising agency in Sydney. Win was an independent woman who took an interest in politics, the economy and current affairs in general. She never married and was known to love animals and children.[4] Win died on 31 July 2002 in Sydney and her ashes rest at the Northern Suburbs Crematorium.

Winifred Vickerman.
SOURCE Sharon Collier

†

1   *Archives in Brief 93*, Background to conditional purchase of Crown land, April 2005, SRNSW.

2   J. J. Matthews, *Good and Mad Women: The Historical Construction of Femininity in Twentieth-Century Australia*, George Allen & Unwin, Sydney, 1984, pp. 148–151.

3   Australian War Memorial, Second Battle of Bullecourt, <www.awm.gov.au/units/>, 2 October 2007.

4   Notes on the life of Winifred Noeleen Vickerman, from Sharon Collier, nee Smith.

7

Adding images

Digital technology is part of every step we take as researchers, writers, editors and self-publishers.

With the aid of a digital camera the copying of documents and other memorabilia in libraries and archives is within reach of most writers and researchers.

Digital cameras have simplified the photographing of landscape, houses, buildings and people because these images now can be downloaded swiftly to a computer for storage, editing and placement into your draft manuscript.

The software that comes with your digital camera or scanner is generally adequate for basic editing tasks. However, too much inexpert work on images can result in bland, dull presentation – if your photograph requires extensive editing it might be best given to a professional.

Read widely and experiment as much as possible, but if you are unsure leave the more technical and complex tasks to your printer, publisher or local photographic expert.

Digital photography

Digital photography has been a boon to the historian, researcher, publisher and writer. You can copy documents, photograph buildings/historical memorabilia and record reunions, meetings, extended family, landscape, buildings, towns and historical landmarks with ease and relative proficiency. Of course all of this is not trouble-free and it has introduced further layers of complexity at the same time as it has provided rich avenues of creative image-making for publication. With the advent of digital cameras, scanners, photo-quality printers and a bewildering array of editing software amateur photographers and self-publishers find themselves thrust into editing and design realms they know little about and which they have, at times, found confusing and difficult to negotiate.

The Internet, too, provides a range of wonderful choices as well as new problems as you access images, download all manner of information and ideas, and then discover copyright/permission issues you should have addressed sooner rather than later.

However, digital technology is here to stay and on balance adds positive and exciting dimensions to our lives. To be well informed about making images and using them in your publication read widely on the Internet, in books and in magazines. Scan articles in popular photography magazines, as these have useful information on the latest compact and single lens reflex (SLR) digital cameras. These magazines will also keep you up-to-date on the release and usefulness of the latest scanners, printers and software. They offer advice on storage of images, image security and archival printing and preservation. Attend workshops or talks on digital photography to improve your camera technique – you will take much better photographs as a result.

Compact or single lens reflex camera?

A compact digital camera (similar to the film compact camera most of us are familiar with and perhaps continue to use) is a point-and-shoot camera. The more recent models have advanced settings and features ideal for everyday low-light or more complex shots. Lightweight compact cameras can be tucked into a pocket or a small space in a backpack and are ideal for travel and for making copies of documents or other items.

A digital SLR has the capacity to take interchangeable lenses and can shoot in a range of file formats such as RAW (the equivalent of a digital negative) and JPEG. The digital SLR has both manual and auto functions enabling the user to manually alter white balance, filters, metering, shutter speeds/exposure, remote control, exposure compensation, bracketing, flash reduction and much more. SLR digital cameras are much heavier to carry and are not as portable as the compact, but they can add much to the quality of your work.

A picture is worth a thousand words … or is it?

Producing a good image on your digital camera does not necessarily mean you must have the latest digital SLR camera with enough megapixels to impress all of your friends and relatives. It is true that an expensive digital SLR camera in the hands of an expert will produce brilliant results. But that same expert will also get pin-sharp, well-composed images on an ancient film camera simply because they have the skill. A few key strategies, however, will ensure that you get good results every time. For those of us creating images for publication, the following is a basic list.

Check your equipment

Many of your images will be produced while travelling or at least away from home, so have a basic list of the equipment you will need for your image-making.

» A digital SLR camera with an 18-200 mm lens will suffice for everyday shots of those distant mountains, background shots, buildings, most landscape shots and family groups. This lens will also cope with indoor staged shots (say at a reunion) or when you can't get close to the action.

» Have at least one prime lens (such as a 50 mm f1.8 or f1.4 lens). This is an ideal lens for indoor shooting of a family group or of individuals at small gatherings.

» Take a lightweight compact digital camera with you wherever you go. A compact is handy for quick snaps when it is difficult to set up or use the larger digital SLR camera.

» Always make sure you have spare batteries, charger, enough memory cards, and a tripod.

Take more photographs than you need

Take more shots than you will need. A friend told me her husband would spend hours setting up his camera and tripod to get that one great shot! A better strategy and one that all good photographers use is to take many, many shots of that event, person or landscape. One in every ten of your shots will turn out to be a great image.

As for the rest, some might suggest you delete them all, but I would offer a word of caution here. All of the images you make are a record of that time, so it is prudent to wait until you download the images to your computer and study them – the background, the interactions, the faces, the various poses – for the large and small moments in them. These images reflect more than that one good image because they tell a story, and a flawed photograph might be worth keeping for reasons other than its sharpness and composition.

Take the best photographs you can

Here are some other strategies for taking good photographs.

» Check if there is enough light on the subjects. Ask your subject to move away from too much shade and avoid the harshness of midday sun. But in the end if you are taking photographs at a reunion or during a visit to an elderly relative just press the shutter quickly and allow the moment to produce the best result you can achieve.

» Consider if you need to use a tripod to ensure the image will be sharp and clear.

» Look at the composition of the photograph. Do you need to ask your subjects to take off their hats, to stand closer together? Try to relax and get your subjects to relax as well.

» Press the shutter quickly and allow the moment to produce a good result.

» Fill the frame! How many times have you taken a photograph only to find that the subjects are too tiny or that one person at the side of the group has a tree growing out of their head? Don't worry – we all do it sometimes.

» Try to take shots with a range of views so that you have many to choose from later.

» Remember that it is important to include the background too. You are a recorder of the moment and that clock or that book or that house or that cup will be important as context when you look at the image later.

Scanning

Scan your family photographs at the highest possible resolution – at least 300dpi but more if possible. The higher the scanned resolution, the better your results will be on the page.

Whether scanning colour or black and white photographs, it is best to scan in colour and preferably from a glossy print. Save your photographs in TIFF not JPEG. Photographs saved in TIFF will not lose quality whereas a JPEG file, as it is saved and changed, will suffer reduced quality over time. You can protect a JPEG picture from additional loss of its visual quality by saving it as a TIFF file. However, ask your printer what format they require for digital photographs and whether they would prefer to do the scanning onsite. With print-on-demand technology now widespread it is relatively cost-effective for printers to insert photographs.

Editing images

Many of your photographs will come from newspapers, books and articles or will be poor-quality prints gathered from family archives. Retouching and restoring these images to improve their production for your book can be done with free software such as PaintShop Photo Pro, Photoshop Elements, Photoscape, Paint. NET, PhotoFiltre, GIMP and Picasa for PC users. For example, in Picasa you can retouch and clone, correct colour balance, redo brightness and contrast, sharpen the image, and strip the colour to produce tones such as sepia or variations on black and white. Most of these programs are relatively easy to use but have more advanced functions for the enthusiast. Mac users should find iPhoto adequate for basic editing and organising of images.

Having said that, it is best to edit your photographs as little as possible before inserting them into your text. Don't overdo it – you will want to retain the historical feel of the images.

For a simple, step-by-step illustrated guide to using the editing functions of Picasa see Susan Fifer (2010) *Family History for the Older and Wiser: Find your roots with online tools*, Wiley, Chichester, UK. And for easy and very accessible lessons on digital photography, scanning and using your computer as a digital darkroom see Kim Gilmour (2010) *Digital Photography for the Older and Wiser: Get up and running with your digital camera*, Wiley, Chichester, UK.

Here are the websites for some software programs:

EHow Digital Photo Editing
   <www.ehow.co.uk/digital-photo-editing/>
GIMP (GNU Image Manipulation Program)
   <www.gimp.org>
Paint.NET <http://paintnet.org>
PaintShop Photo Pro <www.corel.org>
Picasa <www.picasa.google.com>
PhotoFiltre <http://photofiltre.en.softonic.com>
Photoscape <www.photoscape.org>
Photoshop Elements <www.adobe.com/products/>

Choosing paper

Superior quality paper will result in clearer and sharper images on the page. Once again, it will always be a choice between cost (the higher the paper quality the greater the cost) and the detail and quality of the images in your book. Most experts suggest you choose at least 80gsm paper. High gloss-coated paper will provide greater sharpness and brilliance for your images, but the brightness and glare can be annoying for readers. I found the reproduction of photographs in the final printing of one of my self-published books dull and lifeless due largely to the cheaper quality paper (my choice) and the digital technology of the printer. The photographs were bright and sharp on my desktop and when printed with my home printer, but this was not the result from the book printer.

These are some of the difficulties faced by self-publishers and might only be fixed with experience, greater attention to reproduction throughout the process and greater expenditure. There are technical aspects you can pursue to improve your understanding and production of images on your computer monitor (such as calibration) and you can easily find information about this by searching the Internet. Another option is to use average grade paper for your text and a better quality paper such as gloss paper in a separate section for photographs. You can view examples of this layout in good quality art history texts and books which have a number of reproductions of paintings, drawings or sculpture in them.

Inserting images into Word documents

In most instances printers and publishers will ask for the images to be submitted separately. Make a list of where these are to be located on a separate sheet.

If you are inserting images into a Word document (for example, so that you can then convert to a PDF file and submit for printing from file), ensure that your image has been resized and edited as you would like it, then use the *Insert* menu to place it on the page. Try not to resize or edit your image too much before you place it into Word as this will alter the quality of the image. Embed all fonts and images in your Word or PDF file. This will enable those who receive the file to use the fonts even if they do not have them in their computer. To embed all fonts in Word on a PC, go to *Word Options*, click on *Save*, then check *Embed Fonts in the File*. For older versions of Word on a PC you should be able to find this under the *Tools* menu (find *Options,* click on *Save,* check *Embed TrueType Fonts* and click *OK*).

Placement

Photographs can be placed together (perhaps in a middle section of the book) or on the relevant pages where they relate to the text. I prefer the latter, although this is more difficult and often tedious. With the addition of inserted photographs, maps or other illustrations a Word document can become large and unstable. I have found the best way to overcome this is to construct the manuscript chapter by chapter (as separate files). This strategy also helps with layout while keeping the files a smaller size. Place photographs, illustrations, maps or drawings at appropriate places in the text near where there is a reference to them. Look carefully at commercial publications and note how images are placed. For example, a full or half page may sometimes be allocated for one image with generous white space surrounding it, thus providing difference and interest for the reader.

Line drawings/maps

Scan line drawings and maps at a high resolution, at least 600dpi or more to ensure the lines are clear and sharp on the page.

Black and white or colour?

I have a preference for black and white photographs. Sepia images can add an antique effect to page layout although you need to check with your printer re any additional cost. Printing your book in black and white will be much cheaper than printing in colour. Use colour on the cover to improve the look of your publication.

However, if you have the professional knowledge and creative ability your page formatting and design choices might be bolder and more technologically complex. Increasingly, too, the use of colour in printing and publishing is less costly. Ensure you ask enough questions of your printer and understand what options are possible within your budget.

Adding images to the cover design

Keep it simple. I see many self-published family history books with busy covers – too much detail, too many background maps, too many photographs. A simple relevant photograph with a title and author name/s is sufficient.

Write a short description of the book (called a blurb) and put this on the back cover with a photograph, author note and/or other appropriate images.

BookCoverPro <www.bookcoverpro.com/> has numerous examples of book cover designs. It is worthwhile looking at these and also perusing the shelves of your library and local bookshops to see how book covers are being designed today and the range of blurbs and various detail on them.

Captions for images

Not only are photographs visual windows into the past, they are on the first pages we turn to in a book ... *so that is what she/he looked like, ah, so that's the house, the farm, the building*. More than this, the caption tells a further story and we should be as creative, exact and historically accurate as we can be with the captions we add. The following caption from the biography of my great grandmother records the source, record number, donor and as much description so as to identify the date and event:

> Nurse Mary Kirkpatrick. Brooch at her throat. The only photograph of her not in nursing uniform. Probably taken in 1915 around the time of the wedding of her friend Adelaide Cook. Courtesy of Macleay River Historical Society, S/K046, Donor Mrs J. C. Salmond.

The worst thing you can do is to have no caption at all, leaving your reader wondering about the name/s and detail of the image. Each image of a map, individual, house/buildings, farmland, landscape or transport adds to the story but will have much less historical significance if you do not tell the reader or researcher looking at it where it was sourced from and the basic details attached to it. Images downloaded from the Internet are rarely usable for reproduction because they will have a low resolution. In addition, you will need permission to use the image and your caption should indicate ownership/source and its relevance to your text. Many images on the Internet have been sourced from books, libraries, archives or private repositories and with a little research on your part you should be able to establish where originals can be found. Most genealogical and historical societies worldwide have information on their websites on the use and reproduction of images, as do the copyright pages of most government agencies. See chapter 9 of this book for more information.

Keeping your images safe

You collect and then save to your computer large numbers of images, but then face the issue of how to store, preserve and ensure you don't lose them due to mismanagement or a fault with the computer. At the very least you should have a basic system for recording where, how and in what form the images are stored. In addition it is sensible to back up the images on an external hard drive, CD/DVD or USB drive. Printing your material to paper, and/or your images using archival paper may also be an option.

Websites

These websites hold invaluable information on digital photograpy:

Archiving photos to DVD <www.hp.com/united-states/consumer/digital_photography/>

Garvin, Karen S (2010) *How to Print Digital Photos on Archival Paper* <www.ehow.com/how_6372377_print-digital-photos-archival-paper.html>

Gilmour, Kim (2010) *Digital Photography for the Older and Wiser: Get up and running with your digital camera,* Wiley, Chichester, UK.

Library of Congress, *Preserving Digital Images* <www.loc.gov/loc/lcib/08012/preserve.html>

Mitchell, Euan (2000) *Self-Publishing Made Simple: The ultimate Australian guide,* Hardie Grant, Melbourne.

National Library of Australia, *First Steps in Preserving Digital Publications* <www.nla.gov.au/pres/epupam.html>

Electronic and paper publishing

Self-publishing a family story, a biography of a family character, a war story or a memoir is now commonplace, whether we choose to print a book or use an electronic publishing format.

Family and local historians recognised early the usefulness of electronic technology for further sharing their research and resources and for quickly finding others researching the same surnames, family and places.

Family historians and other researchers and writers have been enthusiastic users of email, the Internet, online indexes and electronic devices. It was a logical next step to look for e-publishing opportunities for their family, local and community stories.

However, a physical book remains the most popular format for publishing a family story despite the rise of e-publishing and the release of e-readers such as Kindle and the Apple iPad.

Choosing a publishing format

As a writer you should think about the printing/publishing process long before you finish the first draft. Unless you plan to put your written text in a sealed drawer under lock and key, you will need to think about your potential readers and their expectations of the book. At the very least readers will want to read basic information about the family; its origins, special characteristics, stories about early ancestors. They will want to see maps as well as photographs of houses, people, towns, workplaces and domestic life. As you gather the oral and written sources for your family story, ask family members (who will most likely be happy to buy your book) if they prefer to read a book or if they would read a digital format on a CD or DVD. Would they be happy to read an online version of the family story? Would a photobook be a sensible alternative?

Self-publishing

It is possible to produce a small print run of your family story – say ten, twenty or fifty copies – on a home computer. However, unless you are skilled at page layout, book design, scanning and inserting images, adding images to text, converting Word to PDF, printing, binding and the myriad other tasks associated with the production of a book, it might be best to take your manuscript to a printer.

Printers' and desktop publishers' prices vary, and you need to shop around. Most have an online presence and offer free quotes. Using a local printer or publisher has advantages including being able to visit the printing premises for face-to-face discussions about price, quality and quantities, and ease of pick-up and delivery.

Examine published family histories, memoirs, biographies, local history and other non-fiction books and check the paper quality, size and general layout of the text and images. Note what is written on the spine of the book and the design and presentation of the title and author's name. The following publisher/printer websites offer a range of services from traditional through to e-publishing. In many instances you are able to obtain an online quote, download specific software, find helpful guides for printing and publishing, and you will be able to upload your files quickly to their specifications if you choose to do so. You should look closely at what each one offers, compare quotes and services, and also check with your colleagues within local family history societies and writers' centres before you make a decision.

Booklocker <www.Booklocker.com>
Blurb, a US website with free software
  <www.blurb.com>
Createspace (an Amazon.com company)
  <https://www.createspace.com>
Evagean Publishing, New Zealand
  <www.evagean.co.nz/public.htm>
First Run Publishing
  <http://firstrunpublishing.com>
Infusionmedia Publishing
  <www.infusionmediapublishing.com>
InstantPublisher <www.instantpublisher.com>
Lightning Source <www.lightningsource.com>
Lulu <www.lulu.com>
Outskirtspress <www.outskirtspress.com>

John Kremer's List and short reviews of print-on-
demand and digital printers and publishers
<www.bookmarket.com/ondemand.htm>

State and national libraries offer considerable help and
advice on preparing a manuscript for publication. See
for example:

Library and Archives Canada <www.
collectionscanada.gc.ca/publishers/index-e.html>
Library of Congress, United States of America
<www.loc.gov/publish/>
National Library of Australia
<www.nla.gov.au/guidelines/webresources.html>
National Library of New Zealand <www.natlib.
govt.nz/services/get-advice/publishing>
Publishing in China <http://en.wikipedia.org/wiki/
Publishing in India <www.vpublish.net>

Manuals of style offer up-to-date rules, conventions and
guidelines for publishing, self-publishing, e-publishing,
editing and book production:

Citing Canadian Government Publications
<www.lib.sfu.ca/help/writing/gov-docs-chicago>
Style Manual for Authors, Editors and Printers
(2006), Revised by Snooks & Co., John Wiley &
Sons Australia, Ltd.
U.S. Government Printing Office Style Manual,
online edition
<www.gpoaccess.gov/stylemanual/browse.html>

Talk to as many individuals and organisations as possible.
Your local family history society, state genealogical
society, local historical society and/or local museum and
writers' centres will have insights and information on all

aspects of costing and producing a book. With print-on-demand technology replacing traditional printing, many commercial publishers now offer a range of publishing services for the self-publisher. For information on print-on-demand publishing and how to prepare your manuscript for publication see:

> Article by an Australian author on print-on-demand technology
> <www.spacejock.com.au/PrintOnDemand.html>
> *Avoiding Self-Publishing Mistakes – For Dummies*
> <www.dummies.com/how-to/content/avoiding-selfpublishing-mistakes.html>
> Kimberley Powell's *Publishing Your Family History Book* at <http://genealogy.about.com/od/publishing/a/printing.htm>

Join a local writing group or family history organisation and talk to fellow writers and historians about their experiences with paper and online digital publishing. The better informed you are about publishing possibilities, the more professional your book will be.

Budgeting/costing your book

You will find advice on how to set realistic budgets for printing, promotion and publication of your book in how to self-publish books on library shelves and in bookshops. However, if you and I are realistic about our family history book production, making a profit is rarely a first goal. Breaking even would be a nice surprise, but your foremost aim is to shape and record your family story and get it into print. With digital technology and print-on-demand publishing you can begin by publishing as few as ten copies for close family members and print more copies, in any small or large quantity to suit your budget and your market, at a later date. Price your book so as to recoup your expenses, but set a realistic amount to suit your market/family buyers.

Collections/clippings/compilations

Long before the Internet, online indexes, email and blogging, family historians were compiling their data into attractive books for preservation (combining family stories, precious photographs and memorabilia), as a family record and for presentation to the family. Nancy Gray outlines a textbook step-by-step method for compiling your data into a straightforward collection of documents in her book *Compiling Your Family History*. Many family historians have produced impressive handwritten and carefully decorated family history in heavy ledger-type books, usually illustrated further with pressed flowers, delicately drawn edging and small mementos.

With the aid of computers, printers and scanners these compilations are now sophisticated composites of handwritten stories, typed text, newspaper clippings, scanned documents/maps/images/illustrations, hand-drawn pages, paintings and photography. Traditional and digital scrapbooking and photobooks have taken such compilations into new, innovative and interesting productions.

Scrapbooking

Scrapbooking and the newest endeavour, the digital scrapbook, offer creative ways to publish family stories, reunion memories, anniversary celebrations or the marking of a parent's or grandparent's 80th, 90th or 100th birthday. For an imaginative approach to scrapbooking check out how the Wacom writing tablet converts freehand drawing and graphics into artwork. Most digital photobook services are applicable to scrapbooking. There is a range of dedicated digital scrapbooking software to be found at <http://scrapbooking-software-review.toptenreviews.com>. See also:

> Campbell Slan, Joanna (2002) *Scrapbook Storytelling: Save family stories and memories with photos, journaling and your own creativity,* EFG, Inc., <www.scrapbookstorytelling.com>
> Digital Scrapbook Place <www.digitalscrapbookplace.com>
> Wacom Writing Tablet <www.wacom.eu>

Photobooks/gift books

A range of printing and publishing services is now offered by online photobook publishers. They offer free software on their websites and you are taken through the basic steps of constructing your book, pamphlet or photobook on your home computer. The book is then uploaded to a website for printing to your specifications. Large department stores, stationery outlets, individuals and photobook companies can be found online as well as in traditional shopfronts. Professional photographic labs offer digital printing of photobooks and normally use an online digital printing service such as PicPress or CEWE.

Blurb photo books
   <www.blurb.com/create/book/photobook>
My CEWE Photobook
   <www.cewe-photobook.co.uk>
Family Photo Book (Gould Genealogy)
   <www.familyphotobook.com.au>
Fotopop books <www.fotopop.com.au>
Life Design Books
   <www.lifedesignbooks.com.au/html/s01_home/>
Momento books <www.momento.com.au>
SmileBooks, US <www.smilebooks.com>

Electronic publishing

Electronic or e-publishing is defined as any published medium created, distributed and read in a digital format. The most common formats for the writer of family stories or family history is to publish on a CD/DVD or to a website, blog, one-name site or dedicated genealogy site such as Ancestry.com. It is still possible to print a paper version of any e-publication, and readers and researchers continue to do so ensuring that the paperless office and paperless publishing are not entirely achievable as yet.

Email, mailing lists, news groups, one-name societies and discussion groups constitute an array of electronic methods for finding and maintaining contact with like-minded researcher/writers. More recently social media (Facebook, Flickr, Twitter, LinkedIn and YouTube) provide additional means of communication. Social media also provide a further means of alerting other writers/researchers to your family stories and can link you to the writing and publishing of others. There is also the possibility of iPad, iPhone and Android based digital publishing although to read the family story on a screen 2½ by 3 inches (6.4 by 7.6 cm) might not be a real option for your family readers.

Most e-publishing companies offer free software to format your e-book, or allow you to submit a manuscript formatted in Word as per their style guide. If you do not have the skills or patience to do this yourself, most offer a range of formatting and design services at an additional cost. Read Scott Marlowe's reviews of the latest e-book publishers at <www.scottmarlowe.com/?tag=/self-publishing+your+ebook>. See also:

Barnes & Noble Pubit
  <http://pubit.barnesandnoble.com>
Digital Publishing Company
  <www.digitalpc.co.uk>
EPUB Bud <www.epubbud.com>
Epublishing – Writers Write
  <www.writerswrite.com/epublishing/info.htm>
Familylink <www.familylink.com>
Microsoft Reader <www.microsoft.com/reader/>
RosettaBooks <www.rosettabooks.com>
Scribd <www.scribd.com>
Smashwords <www.smashwords.com/about/how_
  to_publish_on_smashwords>

Publishing on CD/DVD

It is relatively simple to convert your manuscript to a PDF file and save (burn) it to a CD. The cost of postage is minimal and indeed eliminated altogether if the file is uploaded to a buyer via YouSENDIt <www.yousendit. com> or YourFileLink <www.yourfilelink.com>. A digital copy of the family story can also be printed from a home computer and buyers/family members will do so once they purchase the CD or DVD.

Free software such as Calibre can convert a Word, PDF or other file to an e-book format for reading on Kindle or on your computer. You can add a contents page and other data and then save the file onto a CD or DVD for viewing.

Producing a family history DVD and adding music, video, images, text and sound then editing all of this into a professional audiovisual presentation of the family story is a complex task. DVD/video is favoured as a means of recording a reunion, anniversary celebration, 80th, 90th or indeed 100th birthday of a parent or grandparent, and is also used for celebrating the life story of a much-loved parent, grandparent or interesting character in the family. Unless you have the necessary expertise, it may be best to search out dedicated professionals for this task. Look within your local area or city, ask colleagues and fellow researcher/writers and check professional organisations.

Oral history/audio gift book

An oral history can be recorded with a digital recorder, downloaded to a computer and saved to an MP3 file.

The MP3 file is then placed on a CD/DVD, iPod or mobile, or uploaded to a web page for listening/viewing. Recording the stories of a parent, grandparent or other older relative in audiovisual mode captures the nuance of language, as well as the rhythm and tenor of the spoken word. You can add music, song, text and other audiovisual aspects to the recording to produce a rich mix of family oral, written and visual memory. There are oral history associations and museums featuring the spoken word located worldwide. The following is a beginning list. A more substantial list can be found at the website of the International Oral History Association <www.iohanet.org/resources/websites.html>:

Czech Oral History Assocation
  <www.oralhistory.cz>
H-Oralhist <www.h-net.org/~oralhist/>
National Oral History Association of New Zealand
  <www.oralhistory.org.nz/members.htm>
OHA Wiki <www.oralhistory.org/wiki/index.php/
  Main_Page>
Oral History Association of Australia NSW (Inc)
  <www.ohaansw.org.au>
Oral History Society, United Kingdom
  <www.ohs.org.uk>
Principles and Best Practice, Oral History
  Association <www.oralhistory.org/do-oral-
  history/principles-and-practices/>
Yad Vashem – The Holocaust Martyrs' and Heroes'
  Remembrance Authority, Jerusalem, Israel

Blogging

As with the newsletter and genealogy forums, a blog (weblog) is a website maintained by private individuals, societies, organisations and professionals with the aim of sharing information, opinion and ideas on topics of mutual interest via the Internet. Unlike a newsletter, however, a blog is updated regularly, sometimes daily. A blog is a record of one person's daily activities and can also be an account of the family story. Blogs can be both fascinating and tedious. If you are interested in a particular blog you will need to check that site often. Blogs also allow visitors to post comments and interact with others on the site. Cyndi's List has links to many genealogy blogs and the Genealogy Blog Finder should help you locate individuals researching, writing and publishing family history similar to your own:

> Cyndi's List, *Blogs for Genealogy*
> <www.cyndislist.com/blogs.htm>
> GeneaBloggers <www.geneabloggers.com>
> Genealogy Blog Finder
> <www.blogfinder.genealogue.com>

A personal website/posting to other sites

One-name societies, family associations, family/personal newsletters, surname sites, reunion sites and individual websites are many and varied. A website is a useful way of creating an online presence to share family stories, write a blog and alert others to your research. Google and Yahoo will host your website for free, as will Ancestry.com and RootsWeb.com. Managing your own website requires a domain name with web space for the uploading of your files. Purchasing a domain name for a permanent web address (such as writingfamilyhistory.com.au, my domain name) from an Internet Service Provider (ISP) will require an initial set-up fee and a yearly cost. Once you have a provider they will instruct you on how to upload your files to the host site.

Web pages can be created in Word and converted to HTML or PDF for uploading to your site. Most ISPs also offer online tools for creating web pages. Look for HTML editors and WYSIWYG (what you see is what you get) software for ease of use. You can also upload your family tree data to websites such as Ancestry.com and GenesReunited.com. However, be aware of privacy and ethical issues if you are posting personal information about families and individuals other than your own. There has been an upsurge in recent years in the publication of books and websites on how to use the Internet to create web pages for genealogy. The following list will get you started in both creating a family history website and obtaining and understanding domain name registration:

Australian Domain Name Administrator
<www.auda.org.au/help/faq-index/>
Christian, Peter (2009) *The Genealogist's Internet,*
4th edition, The National Archives, Kew, London.
Davis, Graeme (2009) *Your Family Tree Online:*
How to trace your ancestry from your own
computer, How To Books Ltd., Oxford, UK.
Guidelines for Publishing Web Pages on the
Internet, National Genealogical Society
<www.ngsgenealogy.org/galleries/Ref_Researching/
gswebPages.pdf>

New Zealand Internet Service Providers
   <http://dnc.org.nz/story/authorised-registrars>
RootsWeb.com free web space
   <http://accounts.rootsweb.ancestry.com>
UK domain name registrations, with a list of UK
   Internet Service Providers (ISP)
   <www.nic.uk>

Software for paper and electronic publishing

I am often asked if it is possible to use genealogy software to put together a book. Or, indeed, to use other writing and publishing software or online programs now widely available. It is. Recently released genealogy software and other writing software promise to construct a 'book' through a variety of means such as collating charts, sorting family data and perhaps adding a contents list as well as of course the detailed list of names and dates drawn from your research. You can enter biographical details about individuals and generations and create text based on the various charts, family sheets, individual reports, photographs, name lists and other generated set data.

These programs can be useful, and increasingly there is a large and sophisticated number from which to choose. However, *these programs cannot write your text*; nor can they collect your research material and construct a coherent, readable book. In the end it is only the writer who can write, edit, construct, format, rewrite and make decisions about editing and finally publishing the book. Nonetheless, most of us will use a genealogy program as an aid to our recording, storing and indeed writing and publication of our family stories. The following list will help you sort out how such software can be of use to you:

Farmer, Kerry & Kopittke, Rosemary (2010) *Which Genealogy Program?* Unlock the Past, Modbury, South Australia <www.unlockthepast.com.au/unlock-past-publications>

GenealogySoftwareGuide.com <www.genealogysoftwareguide.com>

Software & Computers <www.cyndislist.com/software.htm/>

9

Your obligations as an author

Author obligations can be listed under the broad headings of conventions, ethics and standards. These obligations relate to how we write, what we write about and how we present our writing in a published form. They relate also to our professional interaction with other writers, to our interaction with public libraries and to the presentation and distribution of our books.

Some of the problems facing the writer of family stories – such as personal bias, insufficient evidence and a poor sense of history – can be traced to insufficient attention to our obligations to this wider writing and publishing context.

Writing a family story involves using private information that could be painful for some family readers. It is both ethical and respectful to be sensitive toward the feelings of individuals and their relatives whose stories you are writing and intend to publish.

General standards and guidelines

Whether you are writing a family story, memoir, biography, autobiography, family history or fiction you are obligated to meet certain ethical, moral, conventional and legal standards set by the writing and publishing professions, and by state and federal governments. Most state and national family history organisations have some information on their websites pertaining to standards you should adhere to for publication. For example, the National Genealogical Society (US) and Society of Genealogists (UK) have listed research, writing and publishing standards for family historians on their websites. The National Genealogy Society has a free to download leaflet titled *Standards For Sharing Information With Others*, which has advice of a general nature focusing on copyright and identifying your sources, respecting other's authorship, informing people if you are about to publish family data information relative to them, and issues to do with privacy and ethics. They also advise you to be sensitive to any hurt your publication might bring to any family member:

<www.ngsgenealogy.org/cs/ngs_standards_and_ guidelines>
<www.sog.org.uk/education/standards.shtml>

Journalists, writers' centres, media associations and book publishing organisations all support these standards. See for example:

Australian Society of Authors
<www.asauthors.org>

International Federation of Journalists
<www.ifj.org/en/>
New Zealand Society of Authors
<www.authors.org.nz>
Writers Guild of America, West <www.wga.org>
The Writers' Guild of Great Britain
<www.writersguild.org.uk>

Plagiarism

Plagiarism refers to the copying of other people's writing (no matter what it is) and placing it (pasting) into your own text; that is, passing off someone else's work as your own. Plagiarism also applies if you copy diagrams, maps, charts, photographs, illustrations and material taken from websites and use them without without seeking permission to do so and without written reference to the original source. Acknowledge other people's work that you include in your text by using footnotes or referencing (the following sections on citing your sources and copyright explain this in detail). There is considerable information on plagiarism on the Internet. The following websites offer useful advice, guides and sources:

Copyrights, Plagiarism, and Ethics: Rights to use information <www.ancestry.com/learn/library/article.aspx?article=730>
Plagiarism Copyright Laws <www.ehow.com/list_6860298_plagiarism-copyright-laws.html>
Plagiarism in the Digital Age <www.plagiarism.org>

Citing your sources

With family stories the writer is faced with the complex task of citing many diverse sources from the distant past (such as church, cemetery or land records) as well as those from recent technology such as websites and emails. The rule here is to keep to the main objective of referencing (to inform the reader) with accuracy and reliability. Cite your sources in as much detail as will ensure readers and other writers can find the material easily.

A bibliography lists all of the books, articles, archival, government, oral, family and other material used in your publication. All documents, reports, newspapers, letters, wills, certificates and diaries are listed. In the case of primary source material, the actual location of the material is listed as well. Family story writers are encouraged to attach a bibliography so that their readers, especially other family members and local historians, can locate material they might want to make use of. Here are some brief examples of how you might cite your sources. In a footnote or endnote in a book, article or book chapter the initial or first name is placed first. For example:

> **Books:**
> Kay Schaffer (1988) *Women and the Bush: Forces of desire in the Australian cultural tradition*, Cambridge University Press, Cambridge, UK.

> **Articles or book chapters:**
> Gaye Tuchman (1994) 'Historical Social Science: Methodologies, Methods, and Meanings', in

> Norman K Denzin & Yvonna S. Lincoln (eds),
> *Handbook of Qualitative Research*, Sage,
> Thousand Oaks, CA, pp. 306–323.

Government publications, manuscripts, family papers, newspapers, oral material, downloaded web pages, emails, letters and the myriad other source material the family historian will use to construct a family story is referenced in as much detail so as to enable your reader to find that material if they would like to use it also. For example:

Manuscripts and oral history recordings:

> Admission Registers, Nulla Nulla Public School 1919–1965, New South Wales Department of School Education, New South Wales State Records (NSWSR), 1/3719.

> Allan Kyle, [sound recording] interviewer Rob Willis, recorded with Noeline Kyle, ORAL TRC 5484/86, Oral History and Folklore Archives, National Library of Australia, Canberra, 2006.

> Copyright Application, Allan Henry Kyle and Herbert Clyde Kyle, Series A1336, National Archives, Canberra.

A bibliography is an alphabetic list of all the sources cited in your book. With many people using endnotes these days it might be enough to simply have a select list of the main sources in your work. As this is an alphabetic list, you should place the surname first; for other references the main or most relevant term in the entry appears first. For example:

Books:

Schaffer, Kay (1988) *Women and the Bush: Forces*

of desire in the Australian cultural tradition,
Cambridge University Press, Cambridge, UK.

Manuscripts and oral history recordings:
Kyle, Allan [sound recording] interviewer Rob
Willis, recorded with Noeline Kyle, ORAL TRC
5484/86, Oral.

New South Wales Department of School Education,
Admission Registers, Nulla Nulla Public School
1919–1965, New South Wales State Records
(NSWSR), 1/3719.

As family story writers we collect information from books, libraries, newspapers, articles, bulletins, registers, directories, almanacs, bibliographies, biographical dictionaries, online indexes, friends, family members and much more. All should be carefully acknowledged. Most books on how to write and publish history and family history will provide very detailed and useful advice on referencing and how to construct a bibliography. Elizabeth Shown Mills' work is aimed directly at the family historian and is especially helpful for the novice and the more advanced family historian. Manuals of style (see a list of these in chapter 5) have specific instructions on referencing and bibliographies for various publications, including e-publishing in different countries throughout the world. The following books will help you begin the task:

Lackey, Richard S (1980) *Cite Your Sources:*
A manual for documenting family histories
and genealogical records, University Press of
Mississippi, Jackson, MI.

Shown Mills, Elizabeth (1997) *Evidence! Citation &*

analysis for the family historian, Genealogical Pub. Co., Baltimore, MD, and the website <www.cyndislist.com/citing.htm>.

Shown Mills, Elizabeth (2009) *Evidence Explained: Citing history sources from artifacts to cyberspace,* Genealogical Pub. Co., Baltimore, MD.

Copyright ©

In most instances copyright begins at the time of creation of the writing and ends normally seventy years after the creator's death. Place the copyright symbol © in your front pages with your name and the year; for example, © Noeline Kyle 2011. Copyright requires no formal registration process. If the work is never published the copyright continues indefinitely.

Copyright protects how an idea, information or factual data is expressed (that is, how it is written in text such as in a story, non-fiction book, article, poem, treatise, play, song, novel, newspaper article, set of statistics or table or in a catalogue or directory). If you paraphrase other people's text or ideas in the same way in which the previous author has done you will need to acknowledge that source.

Generally what can be copied verbatim without asking permission from the author (but with acknowledgment) varies. What constitutes a substantial piece of work to be copied will vary depending on what is being copied and from which kind of text. For example, a few lines from a song or a poem may be considered substantial and therefore require written permission from the authors. A rule of thumb: if you use a direct quote from your source material and it is longer than 250–350 words you will need to contact the owners of the copyright and ask for permission to use it. Each country has copyright rules and advice/information on a website. The following list will get you started:

Australian Copyright Council
<www.copyright.org.au>
Canada Intellectual Property Office
<www.cipo.ic.gc.ca>
Comparison table of different countries and their copyright <http://en.wikipedia.org/wiki/List_of_countries'_copyright_length>
Copyright Council of New Zealand
<www.copyright.org.nz>
The UK Copyright Service <www.copyrightservice.co.uk/copyright/p01_uk_copyright_law>
United States Copyright Office
<www.copyright.gov>

Legal deposit

You are required under various state/national acts of parliament to deposit a copy of your book in a national/state library in the state and/or country in which you reside. You should do this as soon as possible after publication. The following websites provide considerable information for the writer and self-publisher:

Agency for the Legal Deposit Libraries (United Kingdom, Republic of Ireland, Scotland)
<www.legaldeposit.org.uk>
National Library of Australia, Legal Deposit
<www.nla.gov.au/services/ldeposit.html>

United States Copyright Office (see the link to
  Mandatory Deposit)
<www.copyright.gov>

International Standard Book Number – ISBN

In general the agency managing CiP (see below) also
organises the ISBN. The 13-digit International Book
Standard Number (ISBN) enables libraries and booksellers to identify your book more easily, and simplifies
the book ordering process for bookshops and libraries.
In most instances you can apply for an ISBN online and
each country/state/county will have a website, which
will also tell you how much the ISBN will cost. See the
following list to begin:

Bowker U.S. ISBN Agency (United States)
  <www.isbn.org>
International ISBN Agency (provides agencies in all
  countries)
  <www.isbn-international.org/agency>
ISBN Australia
  <www.thorpe.com.au>
ISBN Convertor
  <www.isbn-international.org/ia/isbncvt>
Library and Archives Canada <www.
  collectionscanada.gc.ca/isn/041011-1000-e.html>
National Library of New Zealand <www.natlib.
  govt.nz/services/get-advice/publishing/isbn>
Nielsen UK ISBN Agency (United Kingdom and
  the Republic of Ireland)

Cataloguing-in-Publication (CiP)

Cataloguing-in-Publication is a free service offered by national libraries and archives to catalogue all new publications in their country. A CiP provides a record of your book together with publishing information, ISBN and a specific descriptor that facilitates the recording and cataloguing of your book in libraries and bookshops. You will need an ISBN to register for CiP and the following websites will help you get started:

British Library (United Kingdom)
<www.bl.uk/bibliographic/cip.html>
The Cataloging in Publication Program, The Library of Congress <http://cip.loc.gov>
Library and Archives Canada
<www.collectionscanada.gc.ca/cip/index-e.html>
National Library of Australia
<www.nla.gov.au/services/CIP.html>
National Library of New Zealand
<www.natlib.govt.nz/services/get-advice/publishing/cataloguing-in-publication>

Barcodes

A barcode is usually purchased at the same time as the ISBN. You are not legally required to place a barcode on your book. However, it does give a professional finish to the cover and provides, for the bookseller and librarian, the pricing, publishing information, ISBN and CiP data quickly via a scanner.

Public Lending Right (PLR)

Through Public Lending Right (PLR) authors receive a payment under PLR legislation for the loan of their books by public libraries. PLR is generally administered for governments by state or national libraries. You need to register for PLR and you require a certain number of books placed in public libraries to receive payment. This is a free service and could be of some benefit to you. Check out the following websites:

Department of the Prime Minister and Cabinet Office for the Arts (Australia) <www.arts.gov.au/books/lending_rights>

National Library of New Zealand <www.natlib.govt.nz/services/national-collaborative-services/plr>

Public Lending Right (PLR) International Network <www.plrinternational.com>

Public Lending Right (United Kingdom) <www.plr.uk.com>

Index

Your family story will have more value as a published book if you provide an index. Try to index all names of men, women and children. Cross-reference women's names with their original names (previous marriages and maiden names). Constructing an index and correcting it in proof pages is a time-consuming and complex job but will be well worth it. You can also use the indexing function in Microsoft Word, although this is a challenging process and still requires your input to place the entries in their correct alphabetical order. I prefer to stay with constructing an index manually by carefully working through the document to create my entries and sub entries. The author of the text is knowledgeable and should be motivated to construct an index that will help the reader find as many useful entries as possible.

Non-discriminatory language

There is no place in public documents for uninformed, prejudiced or merely insensitive references. Group terms for indigenous people should be checked in manuals of style. The words *Aboriginal* or *Aborigine* are always capitalised. You should inform yourself of the accepted writing terms also for other ethnic groups, women, people with a disability, the aged, young people – and also look closely at your use of naming for other cultures and ethnic groups. When quoting racist, sexist or other demeaning words from past eras or documents you should note that this is a quote and reference accordingly. Avoid using ethnic clichés. Use specific terms where they are known, for example, Nigerian rather than African. Terms change over time and it is sensible to look in manuals of style for current usage. The following websites are a sensible place to start and most government departments will also have other published information in book and leaflet form:

Advocacy for Inclusion Inc
    <www.advocacyforinclusion.org/publications/
    Publications/Information_Sheets/General/
    language.pdf>
Language Portal of Canada <www.noslangues-
    ourlanguages.gc.ca/bien-well/fra-eng/style/

ethnicracial-eng.html>

New Zealand History Online
<www.nzhistory.net.nz/hands/a-guide-to-style>

UCL Human Resources (University College
London) <www.ucl.ac.uk/hr/docs/non_discrim_
language.php>

U.S. Equal Employment Opportunity Commission
<www.eeoc.gov>

Privacy, permission and ethics

Issues related to privacy and ethics have always formed
a part of the obligations of the writer of fiction, non-
fiction, history, memoir, biography and autobiography.
Writers of family stories, family history, memoirs, biographies, autobiographies or personal accounts should
take account of the ethical issues associated with the
use of private material, copying material and distribution of material. Take steps from the outset to observe
the rights of owners of copyright material and of living
people named in documents, and obtain written permission from them for publication.

There are 'horror' publishing stories where individuals have learnt the detail of family secrets for the first
time (those associated with adoption, bigamy, illegal or
criminal activity, separation or divorce, mental instability
and other sensitive issues in past family history) as they
innocently read the story. The shock of finding out in this
way can be traumatic. Most genealogy websites, history
associations and government websites have information
on ethics and privacy for writers and self-publishers. The
library section of Ancestry.com also has useful articles.

There will be family disagreement over what should or should not be revealed about the family. Differences of opinion will arise over adoption, marital infidelity, money, family conflicts, criminality, divorce and separation, neglect, domestic violence, child sexual abuse, sibling rivalry, child physical abuse and other myriad events that impact on families and family relationships. Whatever you decide to write and publish in your family story it must be carefully checked and should never be seen as just venting or be negative stories from one or two disaffected family members. You should also give any disputed text to the individuals who will invariably be affected by that wider publication.

There are legal, ethical, personal and familial issues involved and it is your task to decide if you wish to continue with your version. Some biographers (authorised and not) follow the 'publish and be damned' approach, but if most of your family never speak to you again it might be too high a price for you to pay. All historians must address ethics in their writing and you would be wise to talk frankly to family members if you decide to include data about them or their ancestors that is questionable or debatable.

You should obtain *informed* consent for use of oral interviews. Informed consent requires a permission or consent form to be signed and understood by the interviewee or owner of the material. Oral history associations, history organisations, family history societies and journalists' websites have information on permission and consent for publication. See for example:

Oral History Association of Australia NSW (Inc), Guidelines of Ethical Practice <www.ohaansw.

org.au/page/guidelines_to_ethical_practice.html>
Oral History Society (UK legal and ethical issues)
<www.ohs.org.uk/ethics/>

Defamation and libel

Defamation and libel laws vary from country to country, but there are general principles which can be applied to determine whether persons are being defamed. To defame a person is to make a statement about them which lowers their reputation; and to be considered defamatory it has to be communicated to a third person. Once it is recorded (in any permanent format) it becomes libel. If you write your story and lock it away any defamation arising therein will be irrelevant until such time as that story is published. In some countries it is no defence to claim you did not intend to defame the person or that a mistake was made. In other jurisdictions 'truth' is an absolute defence to an action for defamation. Journalists as well as publishers often deal with issues of defamation and have useful advice on their websites.

Writing a family story or family history invariably includes the research and use of private information that could be painful, harmful or difficult for family readers, and it is sensible to check carefully with your sources for all of the facts. At the same time, if you have any doubts about certain events or facts you should inform the persons most affected and ask them to look over your interpretation of the event. Be sensitive to the feelings of the relatives of the persons you are writing about – occasionally it may be a better strategy to simply leave some stories untold. The laws of libel are unpredictable.

It is not possible to defame the dead but it is possible to defame a living person associated with the dead. The following websites can be of assistance:

Arts Law Centre of Australia, defamation law information sheets <www.artslaw.com.au/legal-topics/archive/cat/defamation/>

The News Manual, a professional resource for journalists and the media <www.thenewsmanual.net>

Getting your book
out to readers

To promote and sell your book, construct a story to tell about writing the book. Tell your readers why, how and when you began writing it, choose attention-grabbing stories about characters and summarise the main conflicts and themes in the story.

Your potential readers will want to know why you were prepared to give years of your life to research and write your book. Show enthusiasm. Be excited and passionate. Take them on a journey as you introduce them to the book and share some of its highlights.

The promotion and selling of your book will require you to give something to your readers. Connect to them by providing insights, advice, stories and ideas through author talks, guest speaking and by offering to take part in community or adult education programs, library events and organised annual festivities.

Marketing and promotion

Your readers (book buyers) will, in the main, be your family, friends, local community and/or a specialised professional or hobby group. Try to balance your marketing and promotion between giving something back (free copies, offering to talk at monthly meetings, donating research material to museums/libraries) and selling the book.

Press release

Write a press release to coincide with a book launch, author signing, author talks, library appearance, media event and for mailing/emailing out to organisations. The press release should be no more than a page. Include a photograph of the front cover and information on the author. But most of all the press release should tell a story about the book. Rewrite your press release to target different audiences – for example, highlight family stories for genealogy, local content for specific places, individual or interesting characters for general readers.

An online press release can be done at PRLog.com (free) or PRNewswire (paid). However, don't ignore your local newspaper, community bulletin and specialist magazines because these are valuable outlets for published family stories whether in e-book or in traditional paper book form, or indeed, both.

> PRLog.com <www.prlog.org> and PRNewswire <www.prnewswire.com> offer ideas for promoting your book online.
>
> Promoting Your Writing <www.writing-world.com/promotion/>. This website has hundreds

of articles on writing, promoting and publishing for an author. It is worthwhile selecting the most useful for your own purposes.

Book launch

Plan your book launch to coincide with a local, regional or other significant event – a regional agricultural show, a significant anniversary (an early ancestor's arrival), the opening of a renovated/restored building associated with your story, a birthday/wedding anniversary or family reunion. Your book launch is also a further means of promoting the book through local newspapers and radio interviews.

Depending on the subject matter of your family story, you can organise a book launch together with an offer of a public talk on the topic of how to write a family story. Focus your talk on offering advice and insights gathered from the writing of your book and relate this to how others can write their family story; in other words, tell them the story of your writing and publishing efforts and send the message: *If I can do it, so can you!* Make this a free event with light refreshments (tea/coffee, juice and biscuits).

Local and regional libraries are possible venues for a book launch as well as schools and a local university or technical/community college. There may be a location, building or place mentioned in your book that is iconic for your story: an old farmhouse, a local hall, the old schoolhouse, a surviving piece of landscape where your ancestors once lived and worked. Often these spaces have meaning for other families and the wider community and it is a good idea to organise your book launch and other promotional activities within this broader context.

Book signings

Contact bookshops for book signing opportunities. Local bookshops are generally willing to host a book signing and will take a few copies of your book to sell later. Sitting at a desk at the front of a bookshop can be a lonely experience. However, I have found that a smile and a friendly hello is often enough for readers to stop for a chat and a look at your book, and will result in some sales.

Author talks/guest speaking

Personal appearances work best for the self-published author. Approach libraries, local organisations, schools and local adult education facilities and offer to talk about your book within their education/social programs. Be flexible with their suggested dates and times. Be prepared to talk for the time allocated. Ask if they would like an audiovisual (PowerPoint) presentation to demonstrate main points and show maps, photographs and illustrations. Ensure the presentation is in the background and refer to it only to illustrate what you are talking about. The main agenda should be your talk and the telling of the family story.

Make sure you include the story of how you came to write the book. Be honest. Your audience will be interested in your writing journey. Have a book table ready for afterwards and offer a discounted price for the participants. Be ready to chat and answer questions.

Online sales

A personal web page and an online order form for your book can help with sales. Participate in discussion lists, online forums and specialist sites (related to your book's topics) and also familiarise yourself with the websites/forums that might help to promote your book. Place your web page and details of your book on Cyndi's List and swap URLs with other websites. Look at Amazon.com, The Book Depository or Publishers Weekly Select and other online sellers for opportunities to advertise and sell your book online:

> Amazon Books <www.amazon.com>. You can sell your book on the Amazon site. You will need a US, UK, French, German or Austrian bank account and Amazon deduct between 6% and 15% commission.

> Cyndi's List <www.cyndislist.com/writing.htm>. Cyndi's List has collected a wide range of advice, information and websites on how to write, publish and promote your family history. This is a good place to start your research on how to go about these tasks for your book. It is also possible to place your own website URL onto Cyndi's List.

> Publishers Weekly Select <www.publishersweekly.com/pw/diy/index.html>. You can submit your book title to Publishers Weekly Select for inclusion in their quarterly supplement, which is distributed to US agents, booksellers, publishers, distributors, librarians and media. There is a fee of US $149, which might place this outside the reach of many self-published authors.

Library suppliers/databases

Register your book with library suppliers and bibliographic databases such as Nielsen BookData. This is a free service and ensures your book is easily accessed by librarians and booksellers. You need an ISBN (see chapter 9) to register. The following websites provide links to library suppliers:

> BookData New Zealand <www.nielsenbookdata.co.nz/controller.php?page=136>. New Zealand authors can list a self-published title here. This is a free service and will help with promotion of your title.
>
> BookData Online <www.nielsenbookdataonline.com/bdol/>, a UK website for Nielson BookData.
>
> James Bennett, library suppliers in Australia, New Zealand and worldwide <www.bennett.com.au>. Register your book with them; James Bennett usually offers quite liberal terms to 'small' self-publishers.
>
> List of library suppliers for UK authors and self-publishers <www.cilip.org.uk>.

Library sales

Design a flyer and email it to relevant organisations, libraries and individuals. Keep in mind that librarians are busy people and reading hundreds of emails with lengthy attachments can lead to a liberal use of the delete button. Use snail mail and bear the cost if you think this would be a better strategy. Send free copies to libraries and to societies you have used for research and also to other organisations and individuals who might promote your book. Non-fiction books, reference books, family histories and local stories are often placed in a specialised local studies or family history section or the main reference section. Therefore, sending a free copy of your book will not hurt your sales and indeed may improve them. Researchers and readers using the book in the library will be encouraged to buy it after use.

Radio interviews

It is often difficult to get an interview on popular radio programs. An email to the program's producer is the best strategy (send them a short press release and tell them why listeners to the particular program will be interested in your book). Always follow up with a phone call. Producers are busy people and you need to be polite and enthusiastic. Don't be put off by a rejection, simply move on to the next radio station. Local, regional and community radio stations are often looking for local content for their programs. Link your approaches to a book launch, book signing or other event associated with your book.

Book reviews

Make a list of newsletters, journals, newspapers, community publications, Internet sites and magazines to send copies of the book for review. Ensure you have the correct name and contact details of the book review editor and send the book to them personally. Attach a short note, not a lengthy letter. Attach a copy of any previous positive reviews or press reports, and a photograph (print) of the front cover of the book. Include interesting prints (of maps, portraits, and so on) from your book and offer to write an article on your book at the same time.

For e-book reviews follow a similar set of steps focusing on getting the attention of readers/buyers online. The following website has useful information on publishing and promoting e-books: Self-Publishing Review <www.SelfPublishingReview.com>.

E-book sales

Both e-book publishers and traditional book publishers will place your book on their website, and include an author profile and link to your personal web page. Some sales will be generated in this way. However, to market and distribute your e-book you will also need to actively promote it via newer technologies such as YouTube and social networking sites such as Facebook. You can place your book with online distributors such as Smashwords, Amazon, Barnes & Noble and Apple's iBookstore.

In addition, marketing your e-book will entail much the same strategies as traditional book promotion. As a self-publisher you need to connect to your potential readers through author talks and by taking part in local library and other community events. There are online versions of these such as Twitter, Facebook, online forums, family history websites and local history events.

If you self-publish a printed book you will already have the manuscript for an e-book (a digital file). However, to sell your book as an e-book, you will need to convert your file to a number of different formats. As e-book publishing is a rapidly changing area of publishing, and there is no single format that works on all e-readers, you will need to do some research into this. At the time of going to press, the most common formats were plain text, PDF, EPUB (the open industry standard, which can be read on many devices including iPad, iPhone, Android readers, Sony Reader, Nook and Kobo eReader) and Mobipocket (for Amazon's Kindle). Free downloadable software, such as Calibre, can convert your file to a range of e-book formats. Wikipedia provides a useful page comparing different e-book formats: <http://en.wikipedia.org/wiki/Comparison_of_e-book_formats>.

Some people say that it is very easy to self-publish an e-book. However, usually those people are already in e-publishing or have been able to master the uploading, formatting, editing, marketing and distribution instructions that accompany websites offering these services. You will need time, patience and considerable computing skills, and must persevere to actually achieve good results. Otherwise, as with traditional book publishing, you will be required to pay a fee for skilled professionals to do the tasks for you.

The following list contains some sources of information for e-book software:

Calibre <http://calibre-ebook.com>. Free downloadable software for converting your book to a range of e-book formats.

Coker, Mark, *The Smashwords Book Marketing Guide* <www.smashwords.com/books/view/305>. Smashwords provide a free PDF file for download from this website with everything in it you would want to know about marketing a book today.

Poynter, Dan (1996) *The Self-Publishing Manual: How to write, print, and sell your own book*, Para Publishing, Santa Barbara, CA.

Poynter, Dan (2009) *The Self-Publishing Manual, Volume 2: How to write, print, and sell your own book employing the latest technologies and the newest techniques*, Para Publishing, Santa Barbara, CA; also available as an e-book from <www.smashwords.com/books/view/607>. Dan Poynter's books, including his latest published in e-book format, cover everything the self-publisher would need to know. He includes, in his latest book, an excellent introduction to all aspects of e-book software, e-book publishing and promoting your book in this growing electronic market.

Stanza, iPhone, iPad and iPod Touch e-book software <www.lexcycle.com>. Stanza is a free application for the iPhone, iPad and iPod Touch and can be downloaded from this website.

WordPlayer, Android e-book software <www.word-player.com>. WordPlayer is a free application for Android phones and downloadable free from this website.

Distribution

Using a distributor for your book is rarely worthwhile unless your book has the potential to sell to a wide audience and you are certain of reasonable sales. Direct sales will most likely be your best selling strategy. If you decide to place the book with a bookshop, try smaller outlets that are more likely to take your book on consignment and charge less commission. Always have a box of books in the car. You never know when you can sell one or two. Country bookshops, especially in towns or regions where your story is located, may take copies and often have a local author stand where you can place the book. These books and websites are worth looking at:

Gawthorpe, Ann (2010) *Write Your Life Story and Get it Published,* Hodder Education, London. Ann Gawthorpe's book is useful because it focuses on writing a life story and the steps you might take to promote and publish it.

The Independent Book Publishers Association <www.ibpa-online.org>. A US website with good information on marketing and distribution for authors.

Marketing Your Self-Published Books <www. crystalreportsbook.com/SelfPublishing_04.asp>. A free website forum with various excerpts from books and published works. This article is useful for the self-publisher.

Using Traditional Publishing to Promote Your Self-Published Books by Ruth Ann Nordin <http://selfpubauthors.wordpress.com> (click on Book Promotion then on the title of this article). Ruth

Nordin is an author and wrote this article to show others the value of using the tried and true ways of promoting a book.

Glossary

alliteration Commencing two or more words in a phrase or sentence with the same sound.

bibliography An alphabetic listing of all sources cited in a publication.

blog Short for *weblog*. A website maintained by an individual or specific organisation as a forum for airing their opinions on a particular topic or theme.

blurb A short description of a book, usually found on its back cover.

caption Descriptive text written to accompany photographs, drawings, maps or other illustrative matter in a book.

CiP Cataloguing-in-Publication. A free service, offered in Australia by the National Library of Australia, that provides a catalogue record for a book, which can then be inserted in the book (often on the back of the title page). The CiP assists libraries and booksellers by providing basic information about your book (i.e. author, title, subject listings and Dewey number).

copy editing The process of carefully reading and correcting each sentence or element of a text for grammar, punctuation, sense, spelling, consistency, style and accuracy. Also called a *line edit*.

copyright An area of law that details the rights of creators of textual, musical, dramatic or artistic works to control their work, preventing others from using those works without the creator's permission.

defamation A spoken statement that lowers the reputation of a person.

e-book A book that is available in an electronic format. E-books can be read on a computer screen or an e-reader, and can be purchased through websites and from bookshops.

EPUB A popular format for e-books that allows the book to be read on a range of compatible e-readers (e.g. iPad, Android, Sony Reader, Kobo, Nook).

e-reader A device that allows you to view e-books. Also called an *e-book reader*.

font A full set of type of one style, such as Times New Roman, Palatino and Arial.

genre A category or kind of literary work, such as fiction, memoir and biography. Also called *text type*.

gsm A measurement of the weight of paper, which stands for 'grams per square metre'. The higher the gsm, the thicker the paper. 80gsm is often considered the mininum weight for text pages of a book.

ISBN International Standard Book Number. A number that enables libraries and booksellers to identify a book more easily, and simplifies the book ordering process for bookshops and libraries. In Australia, these are distributed, for a fee, by the ISBN Agency.

JPEG A compressed digital image format. JPEGs lose quality each time they are edited and resaved.

leading The space between each line of text in a document or book.

libel The publication in a permanent form of material that defames an individual.

PDF A document format that represents the text, graphics and other features of a document, but that can be read reliably on any computer or device with appropriate software.

photobook A printed book created from a set of digital photographs. Captions and text may also be added.

plagiarism To take and use other people's writing (no matter what it is) and include it in your book without seeking permission to do so and without acknowledging the original source.

PLR Public Lending Right. An Australian government scheme that allows authors to be paid an amount of money when their books are borrowed from public libraries.

print-on-demand A digital printing process that allows books to be printed only when an order is received or copies are required, instead of being printed in a large quantity and then stored until they are sold.

resolution (in images) A term referring to the dots of ink or electronic pixels that make up an image. DPI (dots per inch) is one measure of resolution. An image with a higher resolution has a higher level of detail in it than a low-resolution image.

SLR camera A type of camera that allows you to see exactly what the lens 'sees', giving you more control over each image. SLR cameras may be traditional film cameras or digital SLRs, and are generally more expensive than compact digital or film cameras.

structural editing The process of reading and rearranging the parts of a text to improve its structure, flow, sense, readability and user-friendliness.

style sheet A list of spellings and other text styles (e.g. footnote and referencing styles, preferred punctuation, etc.) in a document. Style sheets help writers and editors to make sure documents are consistent throughout.

TIFF A digital image format that retains the quality of the image when it is edited and resaved. TIFF files are generally much larger than JPEGs.

Index